WAL

in

CÔTES D'ARMOR

Northern Brittany

**36 circular walks with maps and directions,
suggestions of other walks nearby
and places of interest to visit**

G. H. RANDALL

Walks in Côtes d'Armor, Northern Brittany
published by Red Dog Books
ISBN 978 0 9557088 3 1

© Red Dog Books 2009

British Library Cataloguing-in-Publication Data
A catalogue record for this book is available from the British Library

Red Dog Books is based in Axbridge, Somerset and in Brittany.
Enquiries should be addressed to the editorial office at
Red Dog Books, 29410 Plounéour-Ménez, France.

email: reddogbooks@orange.fr

www.reddogbooks.com

Printed and bound in China

Foreword

This wide-ranging guide is a welcome addition to the Red Dog coverage of Brittany for walkers of all ages and abilities. Côtes d'Armor, perhaps best known for the Pink Granite coast and northern shoreline, is certainly fortunate in a striking seaboard, but for me the tranquil green heart off the main trails is often more intriguing, an overlooked treasure trove of hidden valleys, lonely megaliths and wild nature. Of course it is this diversity that makes Brittany such a special place, and it triumphs in economies of scale where a rare abundance of contrast in scenery and human imprint is available in a single walk.

The guide presents a beguiling selection of routes, some including famous sites, many others little known and more than worthy of exploration. I have spent much time walking this coast with its stark cliffs, fantastically shaped rocks and exquisite beaches, and am glad to see the fine choice of walks offered here to give more than a taste of these varied aspects, together with an often over-looked appreciation of the economic history of the area.

My own preference, however, is for the landscape of the Argoat, and the book has certainly provided me with many new lines of enquiry in the interior of Côtes d'Armor: I am looking forward to going in search of the Druids' Cemetery at Pleslin Trigavou and the site of an old leper colony near Kermoroc'h.

It is especially pleasing to see one of my all-time favourite Brittany walks included here: you will be hard pressed to find a better afternoon's occupation than following the circuit at Tonquédec with its magnificent castle in a verdant setting. Another exceptional walk I heartily recommend is that at Loc-Envel, with the eerie ruins of Lady Mond's château.

Anyone following the walks in this guide will be well provided with not only enjoyment of many unspoilt nooks of this department but also that sense of potential discovery that lurks around every corner. The clarity of directions and a well-judged degree of enticing background information give all the support necessary for a satisfactory excursion which is relaxing and stimulating at the same time – my personal criteria for a good walk.

Wendy Mewes

Chapel of Ste-Thècle, near Lannion (see page 18)

CONTENTS

ACKNOWLEDGEMENTS

I would like to thank Wendy Mewes for contributing a foreword as well as for her encouragement, advice and expertise. I have found her book *Discovering the History of Brittany* invaluable background reading.

I would also like to thank Lesley Rice for sharing her ornithological knowledge and helping with logistics, as well as other friends and acquaintances who have contributed local knowledge and information.

A word of thanks too for the many tourist officials and administrators whose advice has been of help in preparing this book and last, but not least, the many unseen, anonymous people who regularly and assiduously maintain footpaths and tracks so that others may enjoy them.

ABOUT THIS BOOK

THE WALKS are arranged in three groups according to their length: Short (up to 7kms - colour coded yellow), Medium (7-11kms - colour coded red), and Long (11kms upwards - colour coded blue). The approximate location of each walk and its colour code for length is marked on the department map on the inside front cover. Names for the walks have been chosen to make them easy to locate on any good road map of the department, not necessarily their precise starting point, and they are numbered from west to east within each group. It should be possible to choose a walk of the required length within reach of anywhere in the department.

Some are town walks, some are coastal, some include many points of interest such as megaliths or chapels, whilst others rely on the peace of the countryside for their appeal. Each has a brief introduction to give a clue to what's in store.

In describing the walks, French terminology is used to indicate some features that do not have an adequate English name. Where used, all such terms will be in italics and explained in the glossary on page 10.

Roads are shown on the maps in yellow. This indicates a tarmac road. For simplicity, these are usually shown at a uniform width but of course on the ground they can vary enormously. The more important roads will be 'departmental' roads and will have a 'D' number. Where these roads feature in the walk directions they will be referred to just by their number, e.g. D34. Tracks are marked on the maps by double lines in black, pathways by a single black line. Those to be followed are indicated by a series of broad arrows.

The text directions are succinct and use standard abbreviations, which are listed on page 8. All distances given are approximate - they are there to give an indication of when to be looking for the next turning or the next point of interest.

Historical, archaeological or topographical background

information is given in brown text (and in brown symbols on the maps) to distinguish it from the directions, which are in bold black so as to be more easily followed whilst walking. Diversions or alternative routes are shown in blue, both in the text and on the maps.

Illustrations for each walk have been selected to give a flavour of the scenery to be encountered, rather than to present an image of constant sunshine.

At the end of each walk are indications of other walks that can be followed in the same area, and/or places of interest within easy reach that offer an alternative to walking. Please note that both the places of interest and the other walks are suggestions only and local Tourist Offices or *mairies* may have additional information.

ABBREVIATIONS

CA	Continue ahead	m	metres
D	Route Départementale (eg D10)	R	right
GR	Grand Randonnée (long distance footpath)	PR	Petite Randonnée (shorter footpath, usually a circuit)
km	kilometre	TJ	T-junction
L	left	TO	Tourist Office

GRADING OF WALKS (for guidance only)

Level 1 : fairly level route
Level 2 : fairly level route with gradual climbs
Level 3 : generally up and down, paths needing care
Level 4 : one or more very steep slope and/or many steps

GRADIENT PROFILE

The gradient profiles shown in the heading of each walk are drawn to a uniform scale with sea level as the base line. They can therefore be used to make comparisons between walks, both in terms of the ascents and descents to be encountered as well as their relative height above sea level. For reasons of space the vertical scale is about 7½ times larger than the horizontal scale so the gradients appear that much steeper than they are in fact.

KEY

MAP SYMBOLS

⚑ abbey

✧ archaeological or historical feature

✳ belvedere/viewpoint

⊐ bridge

▬ building(s)

⋏ campsite

† cemetery

✛ château

⸙ church

+ chapel

† calvary or wayside cross

π dolmen

≙ fontaine/spring

⊞ football/sports field

▮ lavoir

⚲ lighthouse

⸫ marsh

⸰ menhir

⚙ mill

Δ monument

∞∞∞ orchard

P parking

⋆ picnic area

① reference point in the directions

⊕ sea-mark

≣ steps

♀ wood

🌲 wood, conifers

GLOSSARY

In the text local words, either Breton or French, are used to denote features whose character is peculiar to the area. Often there is no exact translation but the following is offered as a guide.

allée couverte - neolithic gallery grave

auberge - inn

balisage - way-marking

bourg - village with facilities

centre d'interprétation - specialised museum and study centre - a base for group activities, guided walks, etc.

chaos - river flowing fast through rocks

château - castle or mansion

château fort - castle

chemin creux - sunken track between raised banks

Chouan; chouannerie - Breton, catholic, counter-revolutionary - movement

commanderie - local HQ of a religious military order

commune - local administrative area/parish

déchetterie - public refuse collection point

dolmen - ancient stone tomb

domaine - estate, territory

eco-musée - ethnographic museum aiming to preserve and enhance the natural and cultural heritage of a region

élevage - factory farm, long low enclosed barn for raising poultry, pigs etc.

enclos paroissal - churchyard with architectural features

étang - lake, usually artificial

fontaine - shrine over a spring

gîte d'étape - hostel for walkers

hôtel de ville - town hall

landes - high heathland, moor, with gorse, broom and scattered small trees

La Poste - the post office

lavoir - washing place

mairie - local government admin. office

manoir - manor

marais - marsh

menhir - standing stone

motte - flat-topped mound of earth, originally surmounted by a fort

pardon - festival in honour of a saint

passerelle - footbridge

patrimoine - heritage

pigeonnier - dovecote

point de vue - viewpoint

rigole - feeder channel

ruisseau - stream

sentier - footpath

venelle - alleyway

voie verte - green way, usually a former railway track or canal towpath

Walking in Côtes d'Armor

Côtes d'Armor used to be called Côtes du Nord, a name which better describes its geographical position in the centre of northern Brittany, but which apparently did not please its inhabitants or their elected representatives, who were in favour of a change as early as 1962. In February 1990 the change was finally made to Côtes d'Armor, a curious combination of the French '*côte*' meaning either 'hill' or 'coast' and the Breton '*armor*' meaning 'of the sea' so that one has the sense of 'the land of the sea'. Admittedly, it doesn't translate well but it does encapsulate the department's dual character and sits well with the needs of the tourist industry.

Dual character there is certainly, contrasting the north coast's preoccupation with the sea and everything associated with it from fishing to wind-surfing, with the agricultural pursuits of the *argoat* - the land (originally) of the forest.

There are seven commercial ports, seventeen fishing ports and countless smaller harbours and anchorages along the 350 kilometres of coastline. A coast path, the old

A dry bulk carrier unloading at Tréguier

sentier des douaniers, follows nearly all of it and links the Pink Granite Coast with the elongated estuaries of the Jaudy and the Trieux, the highest cliffs in Brittany near Plouha, the Bay of St-Brieuc, where the tide goes out as much as seven kilometres and pink hued Cap Fréhel where cormorants wheel around the sandstone stacks of *la fauconnière*.

Inland, the other face of Côtes d'Armor is even more subtle and infinitely variable. What at first sight might appear to be fairly insignificant countryside can suddenly reveal hidden valleys and fast-flowing rivers, craggy rock out-crops lurking under a canopy of trees, or strange relics of the past from neolithic alley-graves to wayside crosses and chapels.

To walk through this stimulating landscape is a journey of discovery. In this case, thirty six journeys of discovery, which can be taken on several different levels, according to one's particular interests. Naturalists will want to linger in the deep woods and forests for their ferns, mosses and fungi, by the swampy stream beds in search of the many endangered species that make this their natural habitat, at the bird reserves

of Cap Fréhel, the Bay of St-Brieuc or the Étang de Bétineuc. Historians, with a copy of Wendy Mewes' *Discovering the History of Brittany* in their knap-sack, will be fascinated by the towns - Dinan, Moncontour, Lamballe, Guingamp, Tréguier, as well as by the neolithic menhirs and dolmens, traces of Roman roads, medieval castles and the interwoven stories of wars, politics and personalities. Industrialists can let their imagination play in the traditional linen cloth trade centred on Quintin, Le Quillio and St-Thélo; or the problems of transport between widely spread rural communities, by track, road, rail and canal. Artists can find

inspiration in the legends, culture and traditions of a people whose roots go back to celtic migrations in the 5th-7th centuries and whose creativity is still very much alive. Architecture buffs will be comparing regional styles from one end of the department to the other and across five or six centuries or more. What makes Brittany different, and Côtes d'Armor so fascinating, is that so much of all this remains in the landscape. Population is relatively thin and there has not been any great pressure to develop or exploit every available square inch of land. If a remote water-mill ceased to be viable because transport had improved, it was abandoned. It, or its ruins, will still be there today, as a monument to a bygone age. And if all of this fails to appeal, your day can still be made by the sight of a red squirrel, or one of those spotted toadstools that you thought only existed in fairy-tales.

The practicalities

With all this variety of things to look out for, don't forget the weather; that too can be variable. Always carry a waterproof and an extra pullover, a hat to protect from the sun or the rain or just to keep your head warm, depending on the season. Nearly all the walks in this book entail a variety of paths ranging from tarmac roads, through stony tracks, grass, slippery rocks, earth paths and, after wet weather, mud. It's best to choose footwear that can cope with all of these. Otherwise, walking in Côtes d'Armor is no different from walking anywhere else in terms of equipping yourself. Carry water to drink, and a bite to eat, preferably an energy bar of some description, a basic first aid kit and a mobile phone in case you need to call the emergency services (112). Those are the essentials but of course you can add things like cameras, binoculars, reference books, notebooks, according to your needs and your capacity to carry them.

The Countryside Code applies in Côtes d'Armor as anywhere else. Here is a version that should serve well enough:

Know, love and respect nature and the countryside.
Listen to nature, not to shouting and transistor radios.
Don't spoil nature - it's not a dust-bin - take your rubbish
   home with you.
Don't break branches - respect young plants.
Admire the flowers and wild plants - don't pick them.
Observe animals but don't disturb them.
Don't frighten herds, close gates after you.
Beware of fire, extinguish cigarettes and matches properly.
Stay on the path, don't trample the undergrowth or crops.
Beware of adders: carry a stick.
Don't ignore people you meet, engage them in
   conversation.

Maps

You should not need any other map than the one printed in each walk, however if you prefer to know every last detail, the best you can buy are the IGN (*Institut Géographic National*) *Séries Bleu* at scale 1:25,000. These are roughly the equivalent of the Ordnance Survey pathfinders, though not so detailed and some of the mapping may be quite old or incomplete. Be prepared to follow what's on the ground rather than the map. I have not given GPS waypoints as it really isn't necessary and trying to follow them might prove too much of a distraction. However, I have used a GPS to generate a gradient profile for each walk, a feature that, if studied carefully, a reasonably fit walker will find re-assuring rather than off-putting.

Et voila! Les Côtes d'Armor - bonne promenade!

WALK 1: Ploumanac'h - Pink Granite Coast

Length 5 kms	Time 1½ hrs	Level 1

Location & parking: from Perros Guirec follow D788 towards Ploumanac'h. 50m past sharp left bend by *point de vue*, turn right and follow past campsite to car-park (height restriction - if necessary park at viewpoint).

Gradient Profile

Refreshments: in Ploumanac'h on route, and at La Clarté.

Anyone who has not seen the Pink Granite Coast will find this walk as good as any for an introduction to the splendid rock formations. Pick a clear day, or preferably an evening or early morning, for the best colours and photographic potential - the only problem might be the hundreds of other people who have had the same idea, but there's usually space enough for everyone.

DIRECTIONS

1. From car-park bear left along coast path • At path fork behind big rock, bear R • At path paved with pink granite, CA bearing R past wall • At fork bear L and follow main path (There are many paths and it isn't always easy to pick out the main one. Although many are dead-ends, they lead to good viewing points for particular rock formations. This path system prevents the erosion that results from the many visitors wandering everywhere.)

This is the *sentier des douaniers* - the customs officers' path - and although all of Brittany's coast was patrolled by customs officers on the look-out for smugglers, particularly of tobacco, this section of the coast path is always known as 'the' *sentiers des douaniers*. At a little roofless but gabled building on the right - a former customs officers' hut - look on the left side of the path for the little round look-out with a domed roof • **At path fork go R** • **At TJ go R** • **At Pors Kamor CA past life-boat station** • **CA up towards lighthouse** • **Pass Maison du Littoral on left** *Centre d'interprétation* - information on rocks, nature and wild-life, organised walks • **CA 200m past chapel on L**

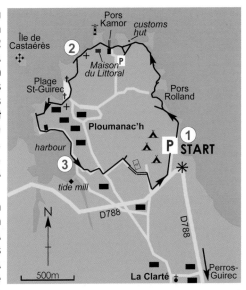

2. Fork L on main path • **Follow away from coast over little hill** • **CA down to cove by cross** (Plage St-Guirec) • **CA around back of cove** • **Pass road, CA to chapel** (Oratory of St-Guirec on beach) • **Climb steps to chapel** • **From precinct bear R through gap in wall** • **CA over rocks and down to earth path** • **Join coast path and go L** • **Climb steps behind big rock, at top bear R** • **At path TJ go L** • **CA through barrier to service road, follow down to harbour of Ploumanac'h** • **Bear L past port office** • **Follow road over little hill and round back of harbour**

3. Just short of tide mill, fork L on Rue de la Plaine • **Follow to TJ** • **Turn R on main road** • **Take first L** (no-through-road, Rue de Ranolien) • **Follow R** (ignoring footpath ahead) • **CA past football ground on left** (ignore marked path left, and another right) • **At road turn R, follow to D788** • **Turn L and follow path on verge to take first L** • **Follow down past camp-site to car-park**

OTHER WALKS in the area:

Trégastel (2kms W) Two walks start from cemetery parking near church: an 11km circuit to the west visiting dolmen, chapels and a ruined château; and a 7.5km circuit to the east along the rocky and wooded Vallée des Traouïero.

PLACES OF INTEREST nearby:

La Clarté (see map) It was the Marquis de Barac'h who vowed to have the chapel built when a beam of light saved him from shipwreck, but it was Rolland IV de Coëtmen, viscount of Tonquédec (see Walk No.25) who put up the money. It's a splendid chapel and usually open.

WALK 2: Lannion

Length 7 kms	Time 2 hrs	Level 2

Location & parking: from the centre of Lannion follow the north bank of the river Léguer upstream, continuing on the D767 (direction

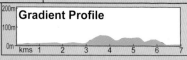

Gradient Profile

Guingamp). At traffic lights by Leclerc supermarket turn right to Camping des Deux Rives. At the entrance to the campsite on the right is a car-park for walkers.

Refreshments: in Lannion. None on route.

This is a short, easy walk, mostly on very minor roads and firm tracks, so a good choice after wet weather. The route follows the left bank of the Léguer upstream as far as the mill at Buhulien, then crosses and climbs to Coat Frec with just a glimpse of the ruined historic château (private property) before returning via Coat Allain with its pretty manor house.

DIRECTIONS

1. **From car-park return to road and turn R • CA 800m, ignore left bend uphill, CA on track beside pumping station • 1.5kms at road follow R over bridge** (in front of Moulin de Buhulien)

2. Immediately over bridge on right is the tiny chapel of Ste-Thècle • **Follow road R, then L, ignoring no-through-road ahead • At fork go L** (ignore waymarks) • To the left, on the wooded hill overlooking the river, is the ruined Château de Coat Frec (private), which was captured by La Fontenelle in the Wars of Religion (see Walk No.25) • **Opposite the farm** (Coat Frec) **take grassy track R • CA 250m, at end descend to another track and follow R • 90m at road bear L • Follow road 420m to TJ, turn R**

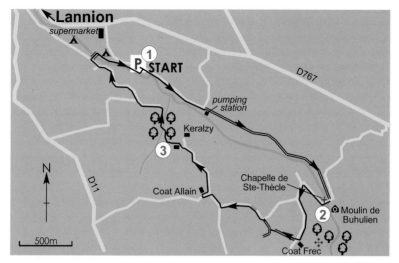

• **125m at junction, turn L 50m to Manoir de Coat Allain on right**
• **Return to junction and turn L on no-through-road** • **500m ignore entrance to Keralzy on right, CA 50m to bear R on path to right of house**

3. **Follow down into wooded valley, bear R at bottom, then bear L across stream, bearing R on other side** • **CA to road and follow it** • **At junction bear R downhill** • **Follow down to river** • **CA 200m then turn R to bridge over river** (within the Camping des Deux Rives) • **Cross bridge and turn R immediately on path following river upstream** • **Follow 400m to road and turn L to find car-park on left**

OTHER WALKS in the area:

Lannion The coast path crosses the Pont de Viarmes in Lannion and can be followed down either side of the R.Léguer.
It also combines into possible circuits: on the north bank, from the Quai de la Corderie (in Kerligonan) to Traou Léguer (7.5kms); on the south bank, from the *caserne des pompiers* (firemen's barracks) in Lannion south to St-Herbot, then west and round to Loguivy-les-Lannion in the north (12kms).
Le Yaudet (7kms W) A 10.5km circuit *Les Vallées du Yaudet.*

PLACES OF INTEREST nearby:

Le Yaudet (7kms W via Ploulec'h) A well-known archaeological site on a peninsula overlooking the mouth of the Léguer. This settlement was destroyed by Vikings in 836 and it is thought that some survivors founded the town of Lannion, while others preferred to go further inland and founded Belle-Isle-en-Terre.

WALK 3: Gorges du Toul-Goulic

Length 6 kms	Time 2 hrs	Level 2

Location & parking: St-Antoine, 2kms west of Lanrivain on the D87 to Trémargat. Park opposite the bar/boutique in St-Antoine.	**Gradient Profile** 300m 200m 100m 0m kms 1 2 3 4 5 6

Refreshments: bar/boutique in St-Antoine; bar/restaurants in Lanrivain. None on route.

The river Blavet is one of Brittany's most important rivers, flowing from just south of Bourbriac to the Atlantic Ocean at Lorient. From Gouarec to Pontivy the Blavet was used to form the Nantes-Brest Canal, although through traffic ceased in 1927 when the barrage of Lac Guerlédan was constructed. The lower reaches of the Blavet are also canalised from Pontivy to Hennebont. This walk explores the upper Blavet at the Gorges du Toul-Goulic, just south of the barrage of Kerné Uhel. The route follows a high level path along the west side of the gorge, with the option of exploring the more difficult route beside the river, where some agility and confidence are needed to negotiate the tumble of large boulders. The return path is up a parallel valley of quiet woodland.

St-Antoine, a 14th-18th century village which was abandoned until quite recently, is now a 'chanvrière' - a site devoted to the production and promotion of products made from hemp (chanvre), ranging from essential oil to building insulation. The ancient granite buildings of St-Antoine are being restored and brought back into use, including a workshop and the bar/boutique. The 15th century chapel is a scheduled historic monument. The site is open all year and visitors are welcome.

DIRECTIONS

1. **From St-Antoine rejoin road and turn R** • Follow downhill past water treatment works and CA over bridge •At end of log rail on left take path L into woods • Turn L immediately and follow R • 100m follow L behind bank then along it • Turn L through gap in bank, bear R and CA • Follow across open ground and CA into woods

2. **After path reaches river** (field visible on other side), **at path fork bear R uphill**

Alternative: fork L here to follow more difficult path near river, eventually bearing R uphill to rejoin main route.

Main route: **CA following path at higher level along valley side • Path from valley bottom joins from L, CA down to path junction**

Like the *chaos* at Huelgoat and the Gorges du Corong (*Walking Brittany*, Walk Nos. 19 & 20), the granite *chaos* of boulders in the Gorges du Toul-Goulic is the result of volcanic action and erosion. 300 million years ago the granite was formed below the surface, which afterwards gradually washed away while tectonic action fractured the solid granite. Rain infiltrated the fissures forming boulders and developing a basin. The river Blavet then carried away the spoil, liberating the blocks of granite, which rolled down the slopes and accumulated at the bottom of the valley. This is what you see today, the river Blavet disappearing beneath the tumble of boulders.

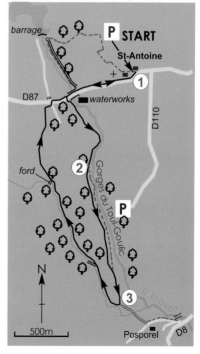

21

3. Diversion: bear L here and follow track to road at Posporel
• Follow road L, follow L at junction, then down to see old slab bridge over the Blavet • Return to this point

3. Main route: **turn sharp R • Follow 1.5kms climbing gradually through woods alongside stream on L** (ignoring track on L crossing stream) **• At ford do not cross but CA on path • Follow up to road (D87) and turn R • Follow road back to start**

Alternative: at water treatment works, just over bridge, turn L through rough parking area and continue on straight track to barrage. Here turn right up hillside and follow signed and yellow-waymarked path to St-Antoine

OTHER WALKS in the area:

St-Antoine For a very short walk, drive to the end of the D110 (see map) and continue on foot down into the gorge. On this eastern side the boulders are even more fearsome and impressive. If you can find it (marked by a blue spot) there is a path that crosses over the *chaos* of rocks with the river flowing audibly but invisibly beneath your feet.
For a 12km circuit around the southern part of the Kerné Uhel reservoir, including the shorter Peumerit-Quintin circuit (see below), from St-Antoine turn left on the D87 and after 200m take the waymarked path on the left.
Peumerit-Quintin (5kms NW) Water, woods and wildlife (birds) are the themes of a 5km circuit around a recently flooded valley adjoining the Kerné Uhel reservoir, 2kms southwest of Peumerit-Quintin.

PLACES OF INTEREST nearby:

Lanrivain (2kms E) The church has a very fine *calvaire* (1548) and an early 17th century ossuary still containing bones (Trémargat, 5km W, has the only other).

WALK 4: Tréguier - town walk

Length 4 kms	Time 1½ hrs	Level 1

Location & parking: Tréguier on the D786 between Lannion and Paimpol. Follow signs to 'le Port' and park on quay opposite twin towers.

Gradient Profile
200m / 100m / 0m — kms 1 2 3 4

Refreshments: plenty of choice.

Tréguier is one of the seven original cathedral cities of Brittany, where pilgrims on the *Tro Breizh*, the journey in honour of the seven founding saints of Brittany, came to pray at the tomb of St-Tugdual, bishop of Tréguier (d.563AD). Besides the cathedral, there is a wealth of ancient religious architecture (mostly with explanatory panels in French and English). St-Yves (1250-1303) the patron saint of Brittany and of lawyers, noted as a champion of the poor, came from Tréguier and spent much of his life here. The writer, philosopher and historian Ernest Renan (1823-1892) grew up in Tréguier and although his work did not always find favour with the local catholic community, his statue is in Place du Martray, right outside the cathedral and his birthplace nearby is now a museum.

DIRECTIONS

1. From parking on water-front take street (Rue Ernest Renan) between towers Les tours d'armateurs, the ship owners' towers, are actually old grain warehouses. Until the quay was built comparatively recently the sea came up to this point • **At top on left is Musée Ernest Renan • CA to Place du Martray • Visit**

cathedral and cloister • Return to Place du Martray and statue of Ernest Renan • From statue, return and pass to L of cathedral around to Place du Général Leclerc behind

The 17th century bishop's palace, now the *mairie*, is at the left corner. A commemorative plaque tells of the 500th anniversary of printing in Tréguier, one of the first Breton towns to have a printshop, where an edition of *La Coutume de Bretagne* was printed in 1485. This was the definitive book of Breton law as established by custom and usage. The war memorial (on right) by Breton sculptor Francis Renaud is considered one of the most beautiful in France.

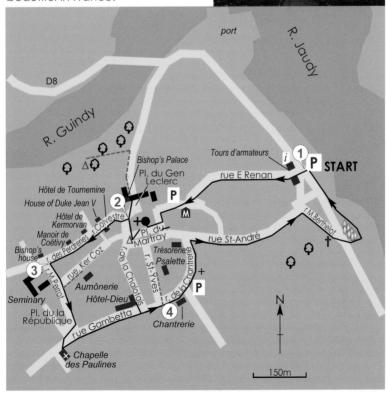

Diversion: go through arch and CA down road 100m, turn L through park gates (Bois du Poëte. The river below is the Guindy) • CA down path 100m to a monument to Anatole Le Braz (1859-1926, writer, academic, collector of Breton songs and stories.) • Return to Place Gen. Leclerc

2. Return toward cathedral and turn R on Rue Colvestre (on left Hôtel de Tournemine, on right, house of Duke Jean V) • **CA along Rue des Perdreries** (on right Hôtel de Kermorvan, Manoir de Coëtivy and Bishops' house)

3. Turn L into Rue Marie Perrot (on right, the former Seminary, now a Lycée, and chapel, built 1894, now the Théatre de l'Arche)

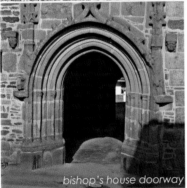

bishop's house doorway

Diversion: turn L into Rue Ker Coz 75m on right, behind stone gateposts, is the Aumônerie (chaplaincy), where lived Abbé Sieyès, one of the leading lights of the French Revolution, when he was a canon at Tréguier from 1776-1780 • Return to Seminary

L'Aumônerie

• **CA across Place de la République, turn R into Rue Gambetta and cross to Chapelle des Paulines** (a teaching order who came to Tréguier in 1760. Their chapel is now a gallery) • **Return and CA down Rue Gambetta** (former Hôtel-Dieu or Hospital of the Augustines on left at corner of Rue de la Chalotais) • **CA on Rue de la Chantrerie to Rue Saint-Yves on left**

Diversion: turn L down Rue Saint-Yves to La Psalette, the choir school dating back to 1443 and now a private house (behind railings on right).

La Psalette Return to Rue de la Chantrerie

4. CA on Rue de la Chantrerie to La Chantrerie on right - originally the home of the *grand chantre*, a top dignitary of the cathedral chapter, it was sold as state property in 1792 but was afterwards used as the presbytery until 1927

La Chantrerie

• **CA past parking on right, bearing L to TJ** (on left corner is the Trésorerie, now the presbytery) • **Turn R** (Rue St-André) • **Follow down to Place du Général De Gaulle and turn R into Rue Marcelin Berthelot** • **CA to the Calvaire de la Réparation** on right at entrance to Parc de la Baronnais

The **Calvaire de la Réparation** (sometimes called Calvaire de la Protestation) was erected in 1904 by the catholic community as their response to the statue of Renan outside the cathedral, which had so outraged them the year before.

Calvaire de la Réparation

• **CA and bear L to water-front to Mégalithes de Tossen Keller**, a group of 58 stones that used to surround the base of a tumulus, c.2500BC, at Tossen Keller in Penvénan, 6kms to the NW

• **Return along water-front to car-park**

OTHER WALKS in the area:

Penvénan (6kms NW) A 9km circuit based on the fishing village of Buguélès combines the coast path westwards with a loop inland between Pellinec and Boutil.

Lanmérin (10kms SW) A country circuit with mills and a chapel links with another based at nearby Quemperven via the gallo-roman bridge over the river Guindy. Details from Lanmérin *mairie*.

PLACES OF INTEREST nearby:

Tréguier Musée Ernest Renan, open April to September.
La Roche-Jagu (12kms SE) Château built in 1405 on a rock above the river Trieux. Château open Easter to 1st Nov, gardens open all year.

WALK 5: Guingamp - town walk

Length 5½ kms	Time 2 hrs	Level 2

Location & parking: entering Guingamp from the N12, follow signs to Parking St-Sébastien.	Gradient Profile

Gradient Profile
200m
100m
0m   kms 1   2   3   4   5

Refreshments: plenty of choice in town centre.

Guingamp is the second largest town in Côtes d'Armor, historically important due to its strategic position at the gateway to Trégor, the region to the north. This ensured that Guingamp featured in conflicts such as the 14th century War of Succession, the late 15th century war that led to the loss of Brittany's independence and the late 16th century War of Religion. But in times of peace the *guingampais* found their position at the crossroads of routes east-west and north-south ideal for trade and the town has long out-grown its medieval straight-jacket, whilst preserving enough of the ramparts to stimulate the imagination.

DIRECTIONS

1. Facing away from river, leave parking St-Sébastien at far right corner, by road going R • At cross-roads CA 80m, turn R to footbridge and cross river to Prairie de Traouzach Some houses bordering the Trieux here have broad granite steps down to the river - these served as private *lavoirs* and were in use until the 1950s. The Tour de Traouzach stood at the west corner of the town walls. To see its remains incorporated into a modern building, take a short diversion to the right, along the north bank of the river **• Follow path L to next bridge and cross • Follow path R along river**

• On the other side of the river is an old *lavoir-sechoir*, relic of the tanning industry, the upper storey ventilated for drying hides • **CA over main road** • **At next main road bear R and CA along left side of river** • **500m cross river by footbridge and turn R to return along opposite bank** • **Past garden centre, cross stream and turn L to road junction** • **Cross two roads coming from right, bear R up steps and CA up sloping path** • **At top CA to right of chapel, bearing L to approach it from other side**

2. Chapelle St-Léonard (patron saint of prisoners)

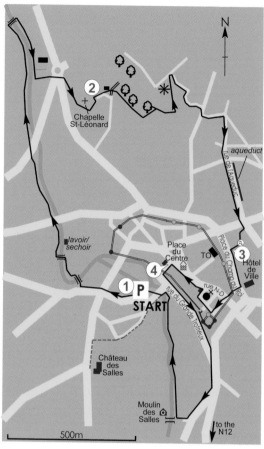

This chapel served as a defensive out-post during Guingamp's many conflicts in the 14th to 16th centuries • **From chapel CA uphill** • **At right bend, CA on narrower path uphill** • **Past house on left, CA across track and into wood** • **Bear R, at first along right edge of wood, cross two other paths and bear L uphill near far side of wood** • **At broader path follow R, out of wood** (There are many paths through this wood and any path bearing R and continuing to climb will do) • **On other side of wood CA across grassy hillside, climbing L** (look behind for fine view of town) • **At upper right corner of open area** (where cul-de-sac ends just below level of main road, see map) **follow cul-de-sac R downhill** • **At TJ turn R** • **50m turn L** • **100m take first R downhill** (rue de l'Aqueduc) • **CA over two cross-roads** After second cross-roads the aqueduct is the stone wall on the left, ending in 4 arches. It was restored in the mid 18th century and supplied water to the

28

fountain, La Plomée, in the town centre • **At main road cross-roads CA but immediately turn R through gateway into park** • **Bear L to bandstand** (1913 - the last one left in Côtes d'Armor)

3. CA 50m to Place du Champ au Roi (opposite library and TO) The name is nothing to do with any real king but refers to a 15th century military game, *le jeu du Papegault* or *Papegai*, for improving the skill of archers and cross-bowmen who had to hit a target *(un papegai* - a wooden or cardboard bird) mounted on the ramparts. The winner was proclaimed 'king'. The tower at this point in the ramparts, which followed the line of this street, was the *Tour du Champ Maurroy* (*maurroy* = false king) • **Turn L, CA 100m to *Hôtel de Ville* on left** Formerly the monastery of the Augustines, who ran the hospital from 1670 onwards, it was built between 1699 and 1709 from the stones of the partially demolished castle • **Cross road to CA down Venelle du Champ au Roy** A plaque marks the site of the 16th century Porte de Rennes - demolished in the 19th century • **Bear R across rue Notre-Dame to CA down Venelle d'Enfer to Place du Château** There have been three successive castles on this site: the first, mentioned in 1120 but probably built around 1040, was a circular, wooden construction on an artificial mound surrounded by a circular ditch 4 metres deep dug from the rock. It was superceded in the 12th century by a polygonal masonry wall built in a style foreign to Brittany but known in England, possibly the influence of the Richmond (Yorkshire) estates given by William the Conqueror to the sons of Eude de Penthièvre. This second castle was rased on the orders of duke Jean V in 1420. He also confiscated Guingamp and passed it to his successors. The last phase is usually attributed to Pierre II (1450-1457) but the archaeology suggests that it was a little later, around 1470 that the castle was reconstructed in a square with a round tower at each corner, designed for artillery. This last castle was never entirely completed, overtaken by the conflicts that led to Brittany's loss of independence. It was finally 'de-crowned', i.e. rased to the level of the ramparts, early in the 17th century because the lord of Guingamp, the Duc de Vendôme (bastard son of Henry IV and nominally governor of Brittany) had conspired against the regent • **Turn R and CA along rue Jean Le Moal to rear of church, Notre-Dame** • **Follow round to front of building and rue Notre-Dame** (visit church if open, or at least the porch chapel where there is a black madonna) • **Turn L to house on corner Maison de la Duchesse Anne**, because her arms used to be above the door, but the renaissance motifs of the facade date from the last quarter of the 16th century • **CA to La Place du Centre and La Plomée fountain** Before being remodelled in the 18th century *la Place du Centre* contained the covered market, the *auditoire* (hall of justice) and the *hôtel de ville*

4. Go L down Venelle du Moulin de la Ville (archetypical medieval street) on south side of Place du Centre - beside the larger of the two fine half-timbered houses • **At bottom turn L on rue du Grande Trotrieux** • **CA under ramparts on left** These date from the 14th century, are three metres thick and were once topped by machicolations (some remain, though filled in, under a modern house built over the walls). The steps on the left lead to the last gate to be made in the ramparts, in the 18th century • **CA past walls, turn R and follow main road down, forking R twice** • **100m turn R into park and CA to bridge** The renovated Moulin des Salles opposite had two wheels and at various times milled either flour or oak bark for tanning • **Turn R along river bank** • **CA to next bridge and cross over to parking St-Sébastien**

Diversion: instead of bearing right into parking St-Sébastien, CA away from river • Fork L up no-entry street • At right bend CA on narrower street • At end CA up passage • At road turn L to find Château des Salles on left • Return same route to car-park

Most of what is visible of the Château des Salles dates from the 16th-19th centuries but it sits on the foundations of a 11th or 12th century castle, complementary to the Château de Guingamp on the opposite side of the river in forbidding passage along the valley of the Trieux. The seigneurial home of the de Kerouartz family and their ancestors, it was for sale in 1999 and was acquired by the *commune*. The little round tower, which appears to be the oldest part, on the right corner of the building was most likely a dovecote.

OTHER WALKS in the area:

Plouisy (3kms NW) A 7km nature trail starting from a former firing range (*champ de tir*).

Pabu (3kms N) A short - 2.1km - circuit between the *bourg* and the river Frout.

St-Agathon (3kms E) A 10km circuit including a manor and a chapel and skirting the forest of Malaunay, refuge of brigands and WW2 resistance groups.

PLACES OF INTEREST nearby:

Grâces (2kms E) The church houses the reliquary of Charles de Blois who led the Penthièvres in their struggle for succession to the dukedom of Brittany in the 14th century.

WALK 6: Quintin - Le Gouët

Length 5 kms	Time 1½ hrs	Level 2/3

Location & parking: Quintin, 20kms southwest of St-Brieuc on the D790 to Rostrenen. From the lake at the bottom of town, drive past the château to take the second on the left, rue des Portes Boulains.

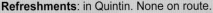

Gradient Profile

At the junction bear right, then take the first left, chemin de la Perche, follow it out to its end and park overlooking the valley.

Refreshments: in Quintin. None on route.

This is quite a short walk but a surprisingly quiet and pretty one, with the added advantage of being close to a reasonably sized town. Take a tour round the château and explore the old streets of Quintin either before or after the walk. Meanwhile, enjoy the free flowing river Gouët, the verdant water meadows and the wooded slopes of the valley.

DIRECTIONS

1. From parking, join footpath and turn R • CA along top right edge of valley (R.Gouët down below) **• At path fork go L and up past a wooden shelter on right • CA down into valley • At path fork go L • At bottom CA towards river, then bear R to bridge** (Pont des Korrigans. Those mythical imps the korrigans have cleverly made their bridge from two concrete telegraph posts and some planks) **• Cross bridge and turn R • Ignore path from left where valley opens out a little with plantation of poplars**

The river Gouët, which flows into the Channel at St-Brieuc, rises 10kms SW of Quintin on the Cime de Kerchouen, a ridge that rises to 318m and is also the source of the river Oust, which flows south towards the Atlantic. The Gouët is 38kms long and drains an area of 240km².

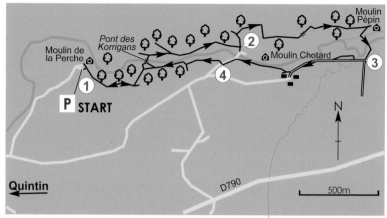

2. At path TJ opposite fence turn **L uphill** • At top bear **L** then follow more worn path **R** • At bank follow **R** • Then follow bank sharp **L** • **CA, descending to follow right edge of field** • **CA through pinch-point, over bridge and up into woods** • Just short of buildings on **right** (Le Moulin Pépin) **turn sharp R and descend** • **Follow L across leet and CA across river** • **CA up through bank to path junction**

3. Turn R on track • **100m turn R onto path across tributary of Gouët** • **CA on path** • At track follow **R** up towards houses • 50m short of road, **turn R onto path beside hedge** • **Follow immediately R and down** (steep slope, loose stones) • **CA down steps to river** (Moulin Chotard opposite) • **CA to road and follow L**

4. 100m turn R onto little path (easy to miss) • **Follow along left edge of field** • At corner of field follow **R**, then **L through gap in hedge** • **CA across field 50m to pinch-point** • **CA roughly parallel with river** • At path TJ turn **R ahead into beech wood** • **100m ignore path R** (to Pont des Korrigans) **CA on broader path and retrace route to parking**

OTHER WALKS in the area:

Quintin A shorter circuit from the same starting point turns upstream from the Pont des Korrigans and re-crosses the river near the sewage farm (*station d'épuration*).

PLACES OF INTEREST nearby:

Quintin The *château* is open afternoons from June to September. There are furnished rooms as well as the vaulted basement.

The Musée-Atelier des toiles de Quintin, a museum of the 17th/18th century linen industry for which Quintin is famous, is open from June to September in the afternoons.

Le Leslay (8kms NW) Château Beaumanoir - 15th century, family home of the notorious La Fontenelle - restored 19th century - furniture, pictures etc. Open mid June - end Sept.

WALK 7: Moncontour

Length 6 kms	Time 2 hrs	Level 3

Location & parking: Trédaniel, on the D6, 1km east of Moncontour. Turn off D6 towards Trédaniel centre - large car-park immediately on right, before *mairie*.

Gradient Profile

300m
200m
100m
0m
kms 1   2   3   4   5   6

Refreshments: in Trédaniel and Moncontour

Part country, part town, this walks starts from Trédaniel and reaches Moncontour via the lonely chapel of Notre-Dame du Haut and a wooded valley approaching the town from the south. Entering through an old gateway, one immediately has a sense of enclosure - this is a small hill-top town that was once surrounded by walls. The walls have gone from wherever they had become an inconvenience in later centuries but the castle remains, tucked away between a bank and the post office.

DIRECTIONS

1. From car-park turn R up road towards church • At right bend, CA on little road to left of church • Follow R around church-yard to TJ and turn L • At cross-roads CA • 600m fork R towards chapel
The Chapelle Notre-Dame du Haut, according to legend, owes its existence to a robbery. An information panel (French and English) gives the full story which, stripped of its supernatural elements, is quite believable. The chapel is often open and has a window illustrating the legend.

Diversion: to right of chapel take 2nd path R and CA down into valley and up other side to *fontaine* • Return to chapel

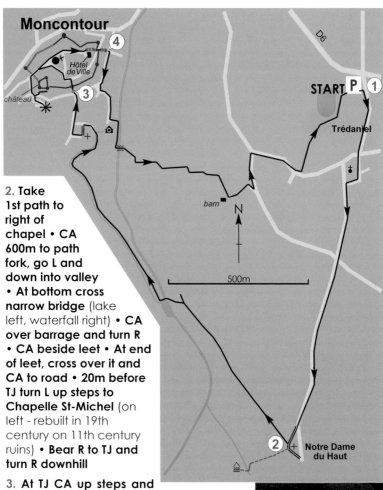

Moncontour

Hôtel de Ville

château

START P ①

Trédaniel

barn N

500m

② Notre Dame du Haut

D6

2. Take 1st path to right of chapel • CA 600m to path fork, go L and down into valley • At bottom cross narrow bridge (lake left, waterfall right) **• CA over barrage and turn R • CA beside leet • At end of leet, cross over it and CA to road • 20m before TJ turn L up steps to Chapelle St-Michel** (on left - rebuilt in 19th century on 11th century ruins) **• Bear R to TJ and turn R downhill**

3. At TJ CA up steps and through gateway • At road turn L, follow R and turn L up no-entry street • In main square (church at near end on right) **bear L to other end of square • Pass post office** (on left) **and note plaque to 'Bras de Fer' in old gateway**

François de la Noue, called 'Bras de Fer', companion in arms to Henri IV and man of letters, died at Moncontour 4th August 1591. As a young man he went to fight in Italy. There followed a long military career - he lost an arm at the siege of Fontenay-le-Comte in 1570, and was fitted with an

Notre-Dame du Haut

iron artificial arm - hence 'Bras de Fer'. He was taken prisoner in 1580 whilst supporting rebelling protestants in the Spanish Netherlands. During 5 years captivity he wrote *Discours politiques et militaires*, which Napoleon later called the soldiers' bible. He corresponded with Sir Francis Walsingham, Elizabeth I's spy-master. In July 1591, wounded at the siege of Lamballe, he was brought to Moncontour for treatment but died here on 4th August, aged 60!

• **Turn L, bear L at junction, then bear R into open area** (from far side good view overlooking the old ramparts) • **Return and turn R down 1st street** • **Turn L up side of Crédit Agricole** (bank) **to see château** The château is sited here to strengthen the weakest part of the town walls, where there is no advantage from the scarp of the promontory, and to guard the nearby gate. It was remodelled several times in the late middle ages, latterly by Olivier de Clisson both before and after being unsuccessfully besieged in 1393 by Duke Jean IV. The town's defences have altered surprisingly little since then, except by degradation, despite its changing hands several times in the franco-breton war of 1487-89, and being taken by the royalists early on in the War of Religion, 1589-98, and held against several attacks until hostilities ceased.

• **Return to main square and CA to left of church** (Rue du Temple) • **CA on Rue des Dames** • **To left of** *Hotel de Ville* **descend steps** (Marches de la Porte d'en Bas) • **At road, cross over and CA down more steps**

4. At road turn R • **CA to open triangle and turn L** (Route du Moulin de St-Michel) • **Follow R and 30m past recycling bins on right, turn L on footpath** • **Follow alongside stream, then turn L over bridge** • **CA, bearing right, up hillside** • **Where path levels out, turn L by remains of stone wall** • **Climb steeply and CA on path** • **At fence, follow R, along left edge of field** • **At green barn turn L** • **At drive, bear R down drive** • **At road turn sharp L downhill** • **150m turn sharp R** • **Follow over hill and in valley turn L on path at back of lay-by** • **Follow down to lake** • **Bear R around lake and up to car-park in Trédaniel**

OTHER WALKS in the area:

Moncontour From la Gare (1km SW) a 8km circuit goes across country to the west and north of Moncontour.

Further walks are based on St-Carreuc (10km NW), Henon (6kms NW), Plémy (5kms SW), Langast (10kms S) and Quessoy (9kms N).

PLACES OF INTEREST nearby:

Moncontour Two museums worth a visit: *la Maison de Chouannerie et de la Révolution*, a museum of the Revolution and Britttany's reaction to it; and *Musée du Costume*, based on theatre and film costumes of all periods.

WALK 8: Lamballe - town walk

Length 6 kms	Time 2 hrs	Level 2

Location & parking: Place du Champ de Foire, near main entrance to Haras National.

Gradient Profile

200m
100m
0m
kms 1 2 3 4 5 6

(NB market on Thursday mornings - parking restricted. Suggested alternative start from point No.**3**)

Refreshments: in Lamballe - at several points on route.

Maison du Bourreau

Chief town of the old duchy of Penthièvre, Lamballe had a castle and town walls until 1420, when they were demolished on the orders of Duke Jean V. The castle was later rebuilt but destroyed again in 1626 - Cardinal Richlieu's orders this time. The large church on the hill, la Collégiale Notre-Dame de Lamballe, was originally the castle chapel and had a dual role as part of the fortifications.

The National Haras (stud-farm) at Lamballe was started in 1825. It keeps approximately fifty stallions to maintain the blood-line of draft horse breeds and holds spectacles and events for the benefit of the public.

DIRECTIONS

1. From entrance to Haras National, turn L • At corner turn L • Bear R past Haras side entrance • At TJ turn L towards church of St-Martin The church dates from the 11th century, when monks from the Abbey of Marmoutiers, near Tours, were established here by Geoffroy Botherel, the count of Lamballe • **At church turn L down Rue des Moulins** (passing back entrance of Haras) • **Past**

Lavoir

St-Martin

lavoir on left, bear L over footbridge • CA, passing to left of sports field • CA to bridge but do not cross • Turn L along river bank • At next bridge turn L (away from river) • 180m turn R, cross car-park and CA to roundabout in front of supermarket • Turn L, CA to bridge (do not cross) Moulin de la Ville on other side. There had been a mill here since at least 1083. Latterly a flour warehouse, and now closed down, the buildings have been converted into apartments

2. Before bridge turn R down Rue du Bief • CA through car-park, cross river and turn L • 150m at TJ, CA on earth path to right of river • Follow L away from railway embankment, into park • Follow L edge of park

Diversion: cross bridge on left to see ancient doorway of the Convent of the Augustines (demolished 1878 and the doorway moved to this spot) • Return across bridge

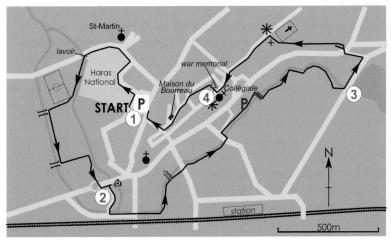

Main route: **CA to road and cross over** • **CA to right of river** • **Bear L over stone arched bridge** • **Turn first R** • **Ignoring road, CA through car-park to far right corner** • **Cross bridge and follow L** • **CA along river** (note private *lavoirs* on opposite bank) • **Through wooden barrier, bear L to road**

3. **Turn L over bridge** • **Turn first L** • **At TJ cross R and CA on footpath bearing left uphill** • **At top pass between Chapelle St-Sauveur and cemetery** • **Bear L on road** • **At multiple junction CA towards Collégiale** (At the far end of the Collégiale is a terrace with a commanding view)

4. **Leave Collégiale by steps up to war memorial** • **Bear L to corner of area** • **Bear L along top of grass bank** • **At end descend broad steps** • **CA down narrow no-entry street** • **Emerging in the square, look behind to Maison du Bourreau** The executioner's house - but formerly called la maison des Bourceau, after the family who built it. They say the name was changed by a photographer who thought his deliberate mistake might sell more post-cards. Today it is the museum of popular art as well as a museum devoted to local artist Mathurin Méheut • **Turn R down Rue Villedeneu** • **At TJ turn R and CA to Place du Champ de Foire**

OTHER WALKS in the area:

Lamballe A 17km circuit to the south and west of Lamballe starts from the sports ground and duplicates the present walk from there to point No.3.

La Poterie (2kms E) A 16km circuit starting from the parking at the NE corner of the lake passed from Point No.3 of the present walk.

St-Aaron (5kms N) From the *mairie*, an 11km circuit to the north of the *bourg* can be extended by 6km into the Bois de Coron.

Meslin (5kms SW) From the church, a long and short version possible, in a figure of 8 between Meslin and Trégenestre.

Noyal (4kms SE) A 10km circuit starting from La Renardière, 2kms ENE of the *bourg*.

PLACES OF INTEREST nearby:

Lamballe Haras National - guided visits in the afternoons, see website for details - www.haraspatrimoine.com

Musée M. Méheut (in the Maison du Bourreau, passed on walk). Open February to December (days limited in low season).

WALK 9: Lanrelas

Length 5 kms	Time 1½ hrs	Level 2

Location & parking: Lanrelas, on the D46 between Collinée and Caulnes. Park near the bridge, by the fontaine St Fiacre and war memorial.	Gradient Profile

(There is more parking up the straight road, to the right of the church.)

Refreshments: in Lanrelas. None on route.

After a short detour climbing to the north, the route descends past a menhir then follows an elongated zig-zag through a nature trail on the wooded slopes above the *chaos* of the upper Rance. Crossing the river it continues to a restored water mill, past a *manoir* with a complicated roof-line, and back into Lanrelas via an avenue of apple trees, each one a different variety.

DIRECTIONS

1. **From fontaine St-Fiacre follow D46 away from town • Cross bridge over river Rance • At cross-roads turn R • CA through Le Rocher** (French speaking map makers wrote what they heard; this village should be '*Rochay*', meaning the possession of the family *de la Roche*) **• CA uphill • Almost at top, turn R onto path • 50m follow R along straight path under trees • 80m bear L and CA through wood** (*parcours sportif* - many of these fitness trails were erected a few years ago to encourage people to keep fit by taking regular exercise, a move which has led perhaps to more straightforward walking activity than the frenetic jogging and stretching indicated by this *parcours*) **• Over hill, fork L by post**

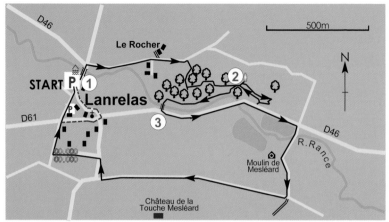

• **CA to other edge of wood and follow path R down** • **50m bear L along bottom of field** • **Re-enter wood and CA** • **150m fork L up to menhir**

2. Return to turn L on 1st path (one above the previous path) **and CA in same direction as before** • **At end, descend through rocks and return along lower path** • **Turn R then follow L to CA** (do not join road) • **Rejoin and retrace outward route briefly below menhirs but fork L downhill** • **Bear L down to river and turn R** • **Various path options through woods,** passing impressive rock outcrops, some with fantastical legends attached) • **CA to footbridge, cross and CA to road**

3. Turn L on road • **700m at crossroads turn R** (to Moulin de Mesléard) • **CA on road past mill** • **At TJ** (with track opposite) **turn R** • **CA 900m into Lanrelas** Château de la Touche-Mesléard across fields on left. Château is rather a grand name for a large manor house. Mesléard is a local name but La Touche occurs frequently in east Côtes D'Armor, meaning a reserve of trees in the centre of an area of cleared woodland • **At junction turn R** • **Take 1st turning L** (before cemetery) • **100m CA on path** (between stone bollards) *L'allée gourmande* or *le verger conservatoire* - apple trees of differing varieties on either side of path • **At road turn R** • **At cross-roads CA down to fontaine St-Fiacre** (or divert R to visit church and village centre)

OTHER WALKS in the area:
Eréac (5½kms NW) A 14km circuit to the north-east, starting from the village centre.

PLACES OF INTEREST nearby:
Langourla (11kms NW) In the centre an octagonal church tower (Historic Monument) remains from the church destroyed in 1869.

WALK 10: St-Germain

Length 5½ kms	Time 1¾ hrs	Level 3

Location & parking: St-Germain, 3kms north of Matignon, off the D786. Park by chapel in centre of village.	Gradient Profile

Gradient Profile: 200m, 100m, 0m — kms 1 2 3 4 5 6

Refreshments: in St-Germain in season, otherwise Matignon. None on route.

From the tiny but once important village of St-Germain - it was a parish until the centre shifted to Matignon when it became a *commune* - this coastal walk overlooks the Baie de la Fresnaye, with distant views of Fort La Latte. Returning up a wooded valley and across country, it revisits a point on the outward route, but then follows a different way back to the start.

This is the spot where St-Germain de Auxerre landed in 429 on his return from Britain, where he had gone with Lupus bishop of Troyes to eradicate the Pelagian heresy by public debate. Pelagius, a widely travelled and erudite Welsh monk, refuted the concept of original sin and asserted man's freedom to choose good or evil. According to Bede, St-Germain and Lupus 'poured out torrents of eloquence' to win the argument.

DIRECTIONS

1. Follow road to R of chapel Built in 1875 to replace the old church but re-using a 12th century doorway and containing a 13th century holy water font, an 18th century altar-piece and various statues from the 16th to 18th centuries. They say that when St-Germain ceased to be a parish the statue of the saint was carted away to Matignon but it jumped off the cart and found its way back here. The harvest is better in the fields through which it passed • **250m at left bend, turn R on track** • **CA on path down into valley** • **At bottom turn R towards ruined mill** (Moulin de la Mer, although it's actually quite a way from the sea) • **Pass in front**

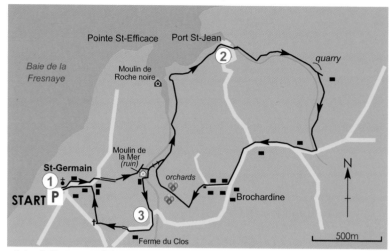

of buildings and turn L • At path TJ bear L • CA 1km following coast path The estuary, with the former tide mill, Moulin de Roche Noire, on the opposite side, is a bird sanctuary

2. At slipway (Port St-Jean) bear R across road and CA on footpath, cross wooden bridge, bear R and CA on path up valley • In clearing with disused quarry on left, turn R onto path • CA (still following stream valley) • At road turn R • At TJ bear R • CA ignoring road on right from Port St-Jean • In Brochardine take 1st road R • At right bend, CA on path (to right of slate-hung house) • Cross field, then CA along R edge of left-hand field • Descend into path between low stone walls • Follow R and CA past orchards, follow R down into valley • At bottom turn sharp L and retrace outward route to mill • CA to L of mill and bear R behind it • Cross bridge above waterfall and bear L past Maison de Lea (ruin) • CA up valley

3. At road turn R • Opposite 1st house on left (Ferme du Clos, with unusual angled stair-turret) turn R onto track/path • At cross, do not join road but turn R onto footpath • CA past houses to road • Turn L and retrace outward route back to chapel

OTHER WALKS in the area:

The coast path can be followed in either direction. See 'Walking the Brittany Coast, Vol 1' to choose your spot. For a short circuit continue from Moulin de la Mer on left bank of estuary to Moulin de Roche Noire and around Pointe St-Efficace to St-Germain.

PLACES OF INTEREST nearby:

St-Cast (3½kms NE) Monument to the Battle of St-Cast, 1758, a defeat for English troops attempting to rejoin their ships after abandoning an attack on St-Malo.

WALK 11: Dinan - town walk

Length 6 kms	Time 2 hrs	Level 2

Location & parking: Léhon, off the D12, 1½ kms south of Dinan centre. Park by the river, either side of the bridge.

Gradient Profile

Dinan - the château and Porte du Guichet

Refreshments: in Léhon, Dinan and at Port de Dinan - plenty of choice.

Taken at a moderate pace and looking only cursorily at the various sights, this walk will take no more than two hours: but that would be to do Dinan an injustice - the town deserves to be enjoyed at leisure. Nevertheless, this walk will serve as an introduction to its geography and some of its history. It also follows a route that avoids climbing steep hills or too many steps. Having done the walk, go back and spend time in the old centre where high quality shops and restaurants inhabit the medieval architecture. Down by the riverside, the port area, in its individual way, is equally attractive.

A little history to set the scene The hill at Léhon overlooks an important river crossing on a Roman road to Corseul but the first mention of a castle here is in 1034. It was demolished in 1169 by Henry II of England. Rebuilt at the beginning of the 13th century, it has survived as a rare example of a castle never adapted for artillery.

The abbey was founded in the 9th century on land granted by Nominoë, who insisted that the monks should have some relics to attract pilgrims. The monks spirited away from Sark (some say 'stole') the relics of St-Magloire, a 6th century bishop of Dol who was buried there, and thus the abbey became L'Abbaye St-Magloire de Léhon.

The name **Dinan** probably derives from the celtic *Dunos Ahna* - the hill of (Sainte) Anne. A wooden fortress, probably on the hill between the port and the later ramparts, protected the valley of the Rance from marauding Saxons and then Vikings. It was burnt in 1065 by William of Normandy (see Bayeux Tapestry). In 1283 Dinan became a ducal town under Jean I who constructed the ramparts on the plateau. In 1357 during the War of Succession, Dinan was besieged by the English and successfully defended by Bertrand du Guesclin. At the war's end in 1364 Jean IV took possession of Dinan and later built the Château. Other improvements to the defences followed in the 14th, 15th and 16th centuries. In 1488 after the battle of St-Aubin-du-Cormier, Dinan was occupied by French troops, following which, as Brittany lost its independence, a period of peace and prosperity led to a developing town, much of which survives. In the War of Religion (1589-98), Dinan was held by the Catholic League but apparently against the wishes of the inhabitants who eventually let in the troops of Henry IV. In the following centuries the ramparts came to be regarded as redundant. Eventually sections were demolished to make way for road improvements until, after the destruction of the Porte de Brest in 1880, the town woke up to what it was rapidly losing, or rather throwing away. The château and ramparts were listed as a Historic Monument in 1886.

DIRECTIONS

1. **From north-west** (Dinan) **end of bridge in Léhon CA up street** (no-through-road) • **Pass abbey on right** The abbey was destroyed by the Normans in the 10th century, rebuilt by the Benedictines in the 12th century, enlarged in the 17th century, and closed down in 1767. In 1792 the buildings were sold to a family who were already living there. (Open in July & August) • **At end of road CA past flower tubs, bear L** • **Join road coming up from right and CA to junction**

Diversion: CA 30m, past road left, and bear L onto path up to château (for an easier way up or down, take road L and follow hairpin right)

Main route: **Turn R** • **Bear L, then bear R up steps** • **At top CA 750m up Rue Beaumanoir** • **At top** (Porte St-Louis to the right) **bear L around outside of town walls** (passing La Tour de Coëtguen, 15th century, La Porte du Guichet, 13th century, and the 15th century château) • **CA along Promenade des Petits Fossés** • **300m, opposite bust of Duclos on column, turn R up steps** (Rue du Fossé) • **CA to junction**

2. **Turn R** (Rue de la Ferronnerie) • **CA along right side of square** A stone tablet opposite commemorates the single combat between Bertrand du Guesclin and Thomas of Canterbury in 1359 during the War of Succession. History is ambivalent about the date, the place or even the purpose of this event, but Dinan has claimed it. The popular version is that 'Thomas de Cantorbery' had imprisoned and held to ransom Du Guesclin's younger

brother during a truce in the siege of Dinan. Du Guesclin rode unescorted to the English camp and demanded his release. Thomas was unwilling to give up his captive and to decide the issue he offered a dual, which he lost and was sent back to England in disgrace, having been made to pay compensation equivalent to the ransom he had demanded • **Turn left before equestrian statue of Du Guesclin and CA on Rue Ste-Claire** • **Turn L in front of Théatre des Jacobins** (Little remains of the Couvent des Jacobins that once occupied this area; it was founded in 1232 and closed at the Revolution) **into Rue de l'Horloge** - visit clock tower (1498) • **Turn L into Rue de L'Apport and bear R into Place des Merciers** • **CA into Place des Cordeliers**

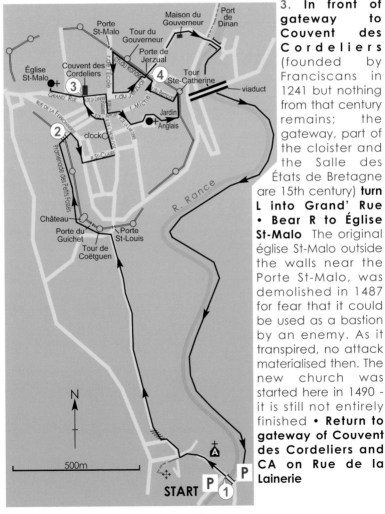

3. In front of gateway to Couvent des Cordeliers (founded by Franciscans in 1241 but nothing from that century remains; the gateway, part of the cloister and the Salle des États de Bretagne are 15th century) **turn L into Grand' Rue • Bear R to Église St-Malo** The original église St-Malo outside the walls near the Porte St-Malo, was demolished in 1487 for fear that it could be used as a bastion by an enemy. As it transpired, no attack materialised then. The new church was started here in 1490 - it is still not entirely finished • **Return to gateway of Couvent des Cordeliers and CA on Rue de la Lainerie**

Short-cut: CA down hill to Porte du Jerzual (point No.**4**)

Main route: **Turn R into Rue de la Poissonerie • Turn L into Rue de L'Apport, then R into Rue de la Larderie • Bear L to La Basilique St-Sauveur** - begun in 1120 following a vow by Rivallon le Roux of Dinan, crusading in Palestine, to build a church in his homeland if he survived • **Visit church or pass either side and CA to Jardin Anglais • On far side of gardens bear L along parapet to top of La Tour Ste-Catherine** (13th century) - spectacular view over river, viaduct

Rue de l'Horloge

(1852) and Port de Dinan • **Return to CA down Rue du Rempart • At TJ turn R down Rue Michel • 40m turn L through iron gateway** (open 9am - 5pm: when closed take next L down Rue Michel and follow down to Porte du Jerzual, point No.**4**) • **CA along Chemin de Ronde** (wall walk: look down through the machicolations and imagine pouring molten lead on enemies below) **past Tour du Gouverneur** (15th century tower for artillery) • **At TJ turn L on Rue de L'École** (Porte St-Malo, 13th-15th century, to right) • **At end, go L down Rue du Jerzual to Porte du Jerzual** (13th-15th century)

4. **Through gateway, CA downhill** (Rue du Petit Fort, passing on right La Maison du Gouverneur, 15th-16th century - but mis-named: it's actually a merchant's house and nothing to do with the governor) • **CA down to Port**

Diversion: stroll L along waterfront and return

Main route: **CA over bridge and turn R along towpath • Follow towpath all the way back to bridge at Léhon**

OTHER WALKS in the area:

Port de Dinan A 14km circuit along the east bank of the Rance to Le Lyvet, across the barrage and returning along the towpath. (outward route recently re-opened after a temporary closure)

La Vicomté sur Rance (6kms NE) A 15km circuit (with short-cuts) from the *bourg* to the banks of the Rance.

Taden (3kms N) From a car park beside the Rance, the towpath and two deep valleys are used to create an 11km circuit.

PLACES OF INTEREST nearby:

Lanvallay (1½kms E) Maison de la Rance, Quai Tallard, Port de Dinan - follow towpath N on east side. *Centre d'interprétation* - nature and environment.

WALK 12: Pleslin-Trigavou

Length 6 kms	Time 2 hrs	Level 2/3

Location & parking: from the D2 Dinan to Ploubalay turn right on the D28, pass through Trigavou and continue to Pleslin-Trigavou.

Gradient Profile

Turn right by church to car-park beyond cemetery.

Refreshments: in Pleslin-Trigavou. None on route.

The "Druids' Cemetery" or "the rock field" (*le champ des roches*) to give it its more prosaic title, is one of the highlights of this short walk. The route also takes in a natural spring, a probable Roman road, a lavoir, the river Frémur and the Chapelle des Vaux with a quaint legend. Talking of quaint legends, the Druids' Cemetery was made when fairies carrying rocks to build Mont St-Michel got tired and dropped their load here.

DIRECTIONS

1. **From car-park, follow park area westwards, descend to minor road and turn L • At junction bear R • Follow L into small car-park and CA on track • 100m divert L into grove of oak trees and megaliths** 65 megaliths in 5 rows, most of them now fallen though originally probably erect, this alignment is claimed to be the 3rd most important in Brittany, though this seems questionable. The presence of oak trees on the site seems to have entrenched the druidic connection in popular culture. True, the oak was sacred to the druids, but the alignment is neolithic, c2000BC, and it is therefore impossible that the druids, who were/are essentially celtic, had much to do with its origins, though they may well have made use of this pre-existing site to perpetuate a knowledge more ancient than themselves • **Return to track and turn L • CA uphill, pass through wood to road and turn R**

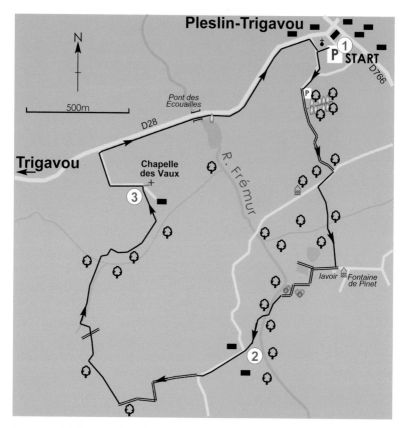

This road is interesting: it is thought to be Roman. There was a ford across the river Frémur at the bottom of the hill and until recently the line of the road could be traced on the opposite hillside. Unfortunately that has now been ploughed out. In the verge on the right of the road, just a little way beyond where this walk leaves it, there is a spring of pure, fresh water issuing from a modern pipe. It is regularly analysed and the results posted nearby. Local people can often be seen filling plastic bottles with this free drinking water, rather than buying similar products in the supermarket • **100m turn L on path** • **Follow down *chemin creux*** • **CA across stream** • **At track TJ turn R** (opposite *lavoir*, now a green algae-covered pond) • **120m bear L with track** (ignore grassy track ahead between lakes) • **Follow R, pass orchard on left, then follow L between orchards** • **Follow R down into woods and CA with river Frémur on right** • **150m turn R and cross river** • **Bear L uphill**

2. At top bear R to road • At road bear L and CA • At left bend CA on grassy track to right of laurel hedge • 250m follow L, then R with field boundaries • **At corner turn R on path between banks • 250m pass through barrier and turn R • 50m follow L • Pass through barrier, cross muddy track** (this too appears to be aligned with the Roman road mentioned earlier), **go through another barrier and CA down path • At stream follow R** (downstream) • **CA over bridge and bear R • Follow L up to field • Follow R field edge**

3. **At road, divert R briefly to see Chapelle des Vaux -** originally a private chapel belonging to the *Château de la Motte Olivet* (1km N from here) but it has since been given to the *commune*. It is dedicated to Ste-Apolline, a 3rd century martyr from Alexandria, who is invoked to cure toothache, reflecting the unpleasant nature of her martyrdom. On a lighter note, this chapel is linked with the legend of the goat that caught a wolf - a panel nearby explains in pictures how it did it. The church at Trigavou (1km W) has some carved beams recalling the event.

Chapelle des Vaux

Return to road • Follow road L • At main road turn R • Follow path beside road all the way back to Pleslin-Trigavou. Just after the bridge, Pont des Ecouailles, is a picnic area with a menhir, said to be an outlying element of the alignment of the Druids' Cemetery.

OTHER WALKS in the area:

Pleslin-Trigavou Two circuits start from the *gîte d'étape* (former station) at Pleslin: an 11km circuit around to the south and an 8km circuit to the north. A further circuit of 9kms starts from the *bourg* of Trigavou and explores country to the west.

Corseul (11kms SW) From the *bourg*, a 13km circuit westwards takes in a ruined castle and the remains of a windmill and re-enters Corseul via the Roman street.

PLACES OF INTEREST nearby:

Corseul (11kms SW) This town (*Fanum Martis* - the temple of Mars) is of Roman origin and has much to show visitors to illustrate its distant past. A complete Roman street is laid bare near the centre, and the *mairie* houses an impressive museum of Roman finds evoking the intense commercial activity of that period. Nearby (2kms SW off the D794) is the actual Temple of Mars - still standing, as the focus of an evidently important religious site.

WALK 13: The Cliffs of Trédrez

Length 9½ kms	Time 3½ hrs	Level 4

Location & parking:	
Trédrez, off the D786 Plestin-les-Grèves to Lannion.	**Gradient Profile** 200m 100m 0m kms 1 2 3 4 5 6 7 8 9

Mairie car-park, just down road opposite church.

Refreshments: *auberge*/crêperie/bar in Trédrez. None on route.

Pointe de Séhar

About a kilometre inland from the cliffs overlooking the vast bay of Grève de St-Michel is the tiny *bourg* of Trédrez. Untroubled by main roads or shops, it has a church, a *mairie*, an *auberge*, a few old stone farmhouses and just enough recent development to remind you that this is the 21st century. It sits on a plateau of farmland 80 metres above the sea, and it's those 80 metres that this walk explores. Most of the way the path follows a line half way up the cliffs, where they become less sheer, but it still involves walking on the edge in quite a few places so please don't attempt it with young children or if you don't like heights. The reward, of course, is spectacular scenery and distant sea views. Across the bay is the triangular shape of the Grand Rocher, while ahead the long outline of Île Miliau off Trébeurden comes into view. Just as you turn to go back there is the peculiar flat headland of Point de Séhar with its precarious fishing village. After the halfway point of the cliff walk there are various opportunities for short-cuts back to Trédrez.

DIRECTIONS

1. From the car-park return to church and turn L • At fork bear L • 30m bear R onto track, follow 650m to Le Rest • At road turn R • 50m turn R onto footpath (ignore track next to it) **• Follow down to road • **Bear L across to path** • **CA on path up to Kerouguel** • **At road turn R** • **At cross** (note 17th century farmhouse on L) **turn L towards Beg ar Forn** • **200m turn L onto track and CA on sunken path** • **Follow down to coast path**

2. Turn R and follow coast path to Beg ar Forn (views across the Grève de St-Michel to the Grand Rocher) • **CA on coast path** • **2kms pass through a pine wood and CA**

Short cut: to leave the coast path take the GR signed path on R in the pine wood and climb to a small road. Follow this R, bearing L in a group of houses, and up to a TJ at point No.**4** on the return route to Trédrez.

Main route: **CA on coast path around next headland, Beg an Evned** • **Follow path R up over rocks** (bit of a scramble with many worn paths) • **At top bear L to continue on coast path** (ignoring path ahead into bushes) • **CA to path TJ and bear L**

Short cut: turn R up grassy track to join road at Lan Charlez, follow R to join return route just short of point No.**4.**

Main route: **CA on coast path a further 850m**

3. Take path (signed) **sharp R** • **120m at path TJ go L** (Alternatively, go R to find the return route 5m away) • **CA** (views of Pointe de Séhar) • **Before first house on L, take path on R** • **Follow right edge of field briefly, then CA on path through scrub** • **Follow 1km to bear L on track, which shortly becomes a road**

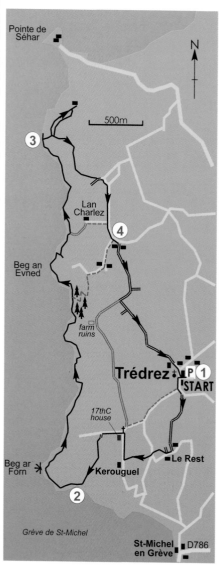

• **Follow road R** (ignore road ahead) **to curved TJ, turn R** • **Follow 500m to Kersalic Braz**

4. At junction bear L • **50m turn R between farm houses onto track** • **Follow 500m** (ignoring first track on left) **around right bend and turn L**

Diversion: CA 350m to see ruined farm on R, and return

Alternative: CA from ruined farm, follow track to road, then, 50m short of cross and 17th century farm at Kerbiriou passed on outward route, turn sharp L and follow road back to Trédrez

Main route: **CA on track** (ignore tracks off to either side) • **At houses track becomes road** • **CA to TJ, turn R to church**

Trédrez

OTHER WALKS in the area:

St-Michel-en-Grève (see map) A 7km circuit departs southwards for 500m then turns inland to Prat Kerleau, NE to Trévinec and returns down the valley of the Ruisseau de Kerdu.

Ploumiliau (5kms SE) A 9km circuit goes around the old lanes (henchou coz).

A 12 km circuit is based on the 15th/16th century churches, including Trédrez, designed by Philippe Beaumanoir of Morlaix.

PLACES OF INTEREST nearby:

Lanvellec (11kms S) Château de Rosanbo, open April - October. www.rosanbo.net

WALK 14: Glomel & the Grande Tranchée

Length 9½ kms	Time 3 hrs	Level 2

Location & parking:	Gradient Profile
Glomel, 6kms west of Rostrenen, on the D3. Park by the church.	

Refreshments: in Glomel. None on route.

The route very quickly leaves the centre of Glomel to find the Nantes-Brest Canal to the north. Following the Grande Tranchée and then the Étang de Trébel, there is a variety of watery scenery before leaving the canal at the first lock on its eastwards descent. There follows the only really up and down part of the walk as one makes for the Étang du Corong. Easy walking along the shores of the *étang* followed by a gentle climb on a quiet road back to town provide a relaxing finish to the walk.

DIRECTIONS

1. From church turn L on main street • 120m turn L (signed 'Canal de Nantes à Brest') **• CA** (ignore fork L) **600m to crossroads • CA on track 650m • At end CA into woods • Ignore cross path, CA up bank and bear R • Follow down steps to canal bridge and cross over**

La Grande Tranchée (the big cut), the highest section of the Nantes-Brest Canal was completed in 1832. Built by forced labour, mostly deserters from the Spanish wars, it took 600 men 10 years to dig. Somehow their misery seems to linger in the sombre atmosphere of this spot.

La Grande Tranchée

2. **Turn R and follow tow-path 2km to road bridge** (D3) • **Climb to road, cross over and CA on towpath, now alongside Étang de Trébel** • **1km at lock, cross by bridge** (pictured on page 53) • **Bear R to cross second bridge then take path on R** • **CA along dyke between Étang de Trébel and Étang de Mezouët**

3. **Over another bridge, CA up path** • **At track, CA up to road and turn R** • **Follow L** (Kergoff to right), **CA to Lopéraré** • **At bend follow L** • **At junction bear R and CA up road** • **Near top turn L** (signed Ar Miniou) • **Follow down to cottage, bear L and CA on path** (initially along edge of garden) • **At road turn R** (the former mill on left, now

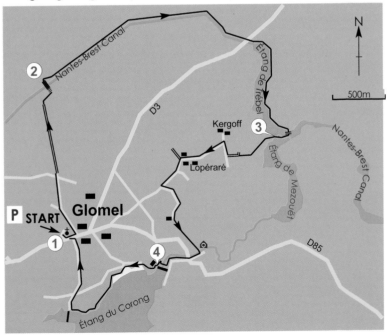

a private house, was working until 1966) • **At crossroads take path ahead** (just to **R** of road ahead) • **Follow through woods** • **Bear R over footbridge** • **CA on path, zig-zagging to top of barrage**

Étang de Trébel

Barrage du Corong

The barrage du Corong, forms the artificial lake, the Étang du Corong, which, together with the lower and smaller Étang de Mezouët, feeds water to the Nantes-Brest Canal. 'Corong' is Breton for 'bathing place'

4. Continue up to bear L in front of cottage • CA on path beside lake • Descend to car-park behind beach, bear L, ignoring all roads, to continue alongside lake • At small barrage on L, CA on road bearing R uphill • At cross-roads CA towards town • At top of road cross to church

OTHER WALKS in the area:

Nantes-Brest Canal The towpath can be walked in either direction from any road crossing - always good for an impromptu linear walk.

Rostrenen (5kms E) The Circuit de Kerbescont (8kms) explores the countryside south of Rostrenen. For a similar walk but including a section of the Nantes-Brest Canal see '*Central Brittany, Coast to Coast*' Walk No.6.

PLACES OF INTEREST nearby:

Coat-Couraval (5kms SE) The gardens *à la française* of the Château de Coat-Couraval (14th century fortified house). Gardens open all year.

Maël-Carhaix (8kms NW) also **Paule** & **Carhaix** Roman Aqueduct (subterranean) details of 'tour of discovery' from local TOs.

WALK 15: Loc-Envel

Length 9 kms	Time 3 hrs	Level 2

Location & parking:
Loc-Envel, 4kms south of Belle-Isle-en-Terre, on the D33b. Car-park on opposite side of D33b from church.

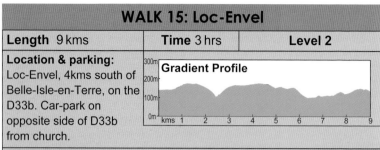

Gradient Profile

Refreshments: Belle-Isle-en-Terre. None on route.

This walk passes a deserted château before wandering through a botanical trail in the 'Forest of the Night' (Coat an Noz). There follows a bucolic ramble by paths, tracks and quiet roads to the 16th century Chapelle Ste-Jeune, returning to the shady valley of the river Guic and a circuitous route back to Loc-Envel. There is plenty of interest - historic, architectural and legendary. Loc-Envel is the smallest *commune* of Côtes d'Armor and the exceptional setting of the church makes it one of the prettiest villages. The 16th century church has a particularly fine carved rood screen and windows dating from 1540, as well as most of its original interior decoration.

DIRECTIONS

1. From car-park cross D33b and take track between houses
• **1km ignore path left into woods** • **CA 300m**

2. Diversion: CA a further 100m to see Château de Coat an Noz, then return

On the site of a fortified manor, the Château de Coat an Noz was built in the mid-19th century by the Comtesse de Sesmaisons for her daughter. It later became the property of the princes of

Faucigny-Lucinge, but was sold in 1923. In 1929 Sir Robert Mond, the nickel magnate, bought it for his wife Marie-Louise Le Manac'h (Lady Mond) an extraordinary character who, despite her humble origins as a miller's daughter in Belle-Isle-en-Terre, was accepted into high society in Paris and London. Since her death in 1949 the château has had

various owners, who for whatever reason have been unable to maintain it. Lady Mond herself found the château too big and had a smaller one built on the site of her father's mill.

2. Main route: **Take track L past second wooden barrier • 10m bear L off track and follow path**

These woods have been converted to a *parcours botanique* with trees identified by name panels (in French and Latin) - some panels may have lost whatever tree went with them, which can be confusing, others mark very young trees which are easily overlooked. These woods are part of a forest that stretches for 7kms across high ground to the east, divided by the River Léguer into the forest of the day (Coat an Hay) and the forest of the night (Coat an Noz).

• **At TJ of tracks** (by seat) **turn L • CA 600m down to road • Cross road and take footbridge over river Guic • CA along L edge of field**

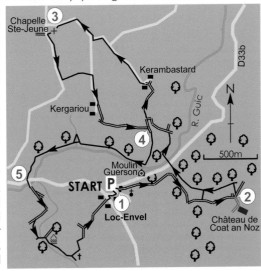

• At corner of field CA into trees • Over first bank, turn R along ditch • 200m at track turn L • CA on track uphill (ignore track R signed Moulin Neuf) **• At second left bend take path R • Path becomes track, follow L towards Kerambastard • Here bear L and CA to road • CA on road** (views on right to Menez Bré, hill with chapel on top) **700m to TJ, turn R • Follow L 400m • Go L through gap in bank to corner of chapel precinct by boules court**

The 16th century chapel is built on the site of Ste-Jeune's hermitage. Ste-Jeune was the sister of St-Envel: according to some

Chapelle Ste-Jeune

versions of their story there were two brothers, both called Envel and both abbots, while their sister also was in holy orders. They left Wales to flee the advancing Saxons and settled in this area where each set up a hermitage. (If you follow the two brothers version the other hermitage has been replaced by the Chapelle du Bois in Belle-Isle-en-Terre). St-Envel and Ste-Jeune had vowed not to meet unless separated by water and therefore they were in the habit of conversing across the river Guic. There is a legend that one day when the river was in flood and rushing noisily over the rocks St-Envel could not hear his sister speak so commanded the river to be silent, since when it has never raised its voice.

3. Cross to far corner of chapel precinct, turn L on road • 450m turn L onto path (by *lavoir*) **• CA to road, turn R • CA to Kergariou, follow around first R bend then bear L on track • 200m follow R then L • Follow stony track downhill** (views of Loc-Envel to right)

4. At TJ turn R on grassy track • Follow L edge of field then CA on narrow path down to river Guic (opposite Moulin Guerson, a former flour mill, later a sawmill that used to generate electricity for the château and the village - one 25watt bulb per house) **• Follow path R alongside river • 600m follow R uphill • Bear L through signed gap in bank • On opposite side of little valley, join path coming from right and CA to road**

5. Cross to road opposite and CA over bridge • Here road becomes stony track • 70m follow uphill (ignore track L into fish farm) **then follow R • Before top, bear L onto path downhill • Follow alongside river (Ruisseau de Lan Scalon) • At path TJ turn L and go over footbridge • On other side turn R onto path by large horizontal rock** (good seat) • **CA** past fontaine marked by three menhirs • **At 3-way path junction bear L uphill** (oratory of St-Sébastien here) • **At field bear L along L edge • Follow R**

Oratory of St-Sébastien

between fields • Path becomes a track • At another track coming from L, bear R and follow to road • Turn L on road • 50m at stop-sign turn R and follow down to start

OTHER WALKS in the area:

Loc-Envel A 6km walk in open country to the south of the village, *Sentier des Landes* - start by the church.

A 10km walk in the forest of the night - start at the *Site des Vieilles Forges* 1km along D33b towards Belle-Isle-en-Terre.

Belle-Isle-en-Terre (4kms N) A 10km circuit out to the remains of the Kernansquillec barrage on the river Léguer, passing sites of former paper mills - start Place de la Mairie - out by GR34a, return by PR through Kergadalen.

For a long walk, 23kms, start at the *Salle de Fêtes* near the church, follow the GR34a south to the Chapelle Ste-Jeune, follow our route from there round to point 2, from there stay on the track down to *Site des Vieilles Forges* on the D33b and follow forest walk to River Léguer, then take the PR back to Belle-Isle.

Plougonver (5kms S) 7km country walk - start at the sports ground on the D54 to Gurunhuel.

PLACES OF INTEREST nearby:

Belle-Isle-en-Terre (4kms N) *Le Conservatoire de la Lutte Bretonne et des Jeux Bretons* in the left wing of the *mairie* is a museum of Breton wrestling (*Gouren*) and Breton games.

Length 10½ kms	Time 3 hrs	Level 3

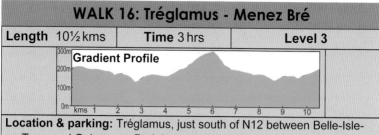

Gradient Profile

Location & parking: Tréglamus, just south of N12 between Belle-Isle-en-Terre and Guingamp. Park in centre near church.

Refreshments: bar and bar/café in Tréglamus, otherwise Louargat (4kms W). None on route

This walk has a very definite goal - the chapel of St-Hervé at the summit of Menez Bré. At 302 metres it has a panoramic view of Côtes d'Armor and has been a focal meeting point since the 6th century when, according to some versions of the story, the blind St-Hervé chose it as a suitable place to hear the case against the notorious Conomor. Fairs have been held here since medieval times until as recently as the 1960s. The walk starts from Tréglamus and crosses the N12 painlessly by a bridge on the way out and a tunnel on the way back. It also crosses the youthful River Jaudy, both times by a footbridge next to a ford. Most of the route is by well-maintained farm tracks and the climb to the top of Menez Bré is fairly steady by the chosen route.

DIRECTIONS

1. **From church walk up road opposite** (signed Gurunhuel) • **200m,** opposite *mairie*, before R bend, **turn L • At end of road CA on path** (ignore path R) • **Follow down to TJ with track, turn R on grassy track • At barn on L turn L to road • Turn R, 50m turn L • At end of road CA on path • Ignore path to L, CA • At track turn R • CA to TJ, turn L • Follow down to main road and turn R • Follow 350m, turn L**

2. CA over N12 (bridge) **and turn sharp L immediately onto track • Follow R, away from N12 • CA on track 350m • Turn R onto larger track** (climb steps onto L bank if track too muddy) **down to ford over river Jaudy • Cross by footbridge and CA up track** (note ruins of mill on right and a few metres later the track crosses the leet, still in water) **• CA uphill to hamlet (St-Efflam) • At road CA to junction and CA up to cross-roads**

3. CA on stony road • Follow 500m, fork R • CA to Kerbré • At road by cross, bear L • 50m follow L • 50m fork L • 130m fork R (ignore *balisage*) **• CA to junction and bear L ahead uphill • CA up to track TJ**

4. Turn L and CA on grassy track • 450m at car-park, turn L on road and cross to chapel of St-Hervé • From chapel porch, turn L along hedgerow opposite • Take second path on R (still only about 50m from chapel) **• Follow wide grassy path 800m down to road and turn L • At junction bear R • CA 100m to staggered crossroads** (both R and L are No-Through-Roads) **• CA** (signed St-Brieuc) **follow under N12 to TJ • Turn L • 50m turn sharp R onto stony road • Follow L to hamlet (Hent Guer Meur)**

5. At road turn L onto track • At cross tracks CA • Follow main track (ignore track L) **down to ford across river Jaudy • Cross by**

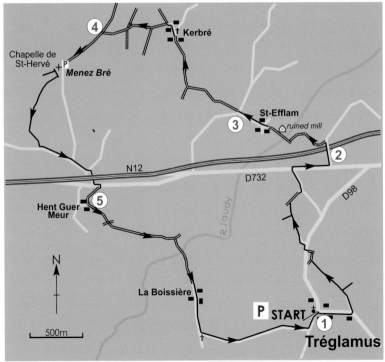

River Jaudy

footbridge and CA • CA on road past farm (La Boissière) • At junction by cross (interesting double cross with armorial shields on underside of lower cross) turn L • Follow to TJ turn L • Follow into Tréglamus

OTHER WALKS in the area:

Louargat (7kms W) Although in the *commune* of Louargat, the starting point at 'Poull Pri' is actually nearer to Gurunhuel (9kms S from Tréglamus). From the entrance to the forest 'Coat an Hay' a 14 km 5hr circuit goes round the forest and some of the country to its north.

Gurunhuel (9kms S) A 9km circuit 'from the top to the bottom of the valley' through country steeped in spirituality and legend. Start at the *mairie*.

A curious double cross

PLACES OF INTEREST nearby:

Pédernec (6kms N) The church has a fine stained-glass window depicting the scene on Menez Bré when the evil Conomor was judged and excommunicated.

Louargat (7kms W) The Menhir de Pergat (off the D31 2kms north of Louargat) is the fourth largest in Europe at 10m high and 12.5m circumference at its base. There is a smaller menhir nearby. Also in Louargat, the spherical Stèle St-Michel (iron age) and the Stèle Gauloise de Crec'h Even, pierced with 11 holes (500-450BC).

WALK 17: Plougrescant

Length 10 kms	Time 3 hrs	Level 2/3

Location & parking: Plougrescant on D8 north of Tréguier. Continue beyond chapel of St-Gonery to park in Place de la Mairie on right.

Gradient Profile

Refreshments: baker/*salon du thé* in Place de la Mairie. None on route except at end in Plougrescant.

Plougrescant, in the middle of the peninsula north of Tréguier and west of the Jaudy estuary, is the starting point for this coastal walk around the Pointe du Château. There is no castle there but there are some impressive rocks that require only a little imagination to transform them into fairy-tale castles or medieval fortresses. The seascape changes constantly as craggy off-shore rocks are revealed or hidden by the tide, caught in an elusive ray of sunlight or rendered dark and forbidding by a passing cloud, while the sea frolics around them with foamy abandon.

DIRECTIONS

1. **From Place de la Mairie turn L on road, return to chapel and turn L • 200m fork R • 500m at TJ** (driveway to Château Kergrec'h ahead) **turn L • 200m at TJ turn R • 400m at TJ turn sharp R • Downhill follow L and CA 450m to TJ • Turn R and fork R immediately • CA down to shore**

2. **Turn L onto coast path to right of fence around oyster sheds • Follow 300m, descend R to car-park and port area • CA through car-park to road • turn L and immediately R up steps on bank to CA on coast path • At road follow R of cottage and CA on coast path • 600m follow path inland • CA up R edge of field • Bear R**

onto road • At TJ go R • At fork bear R downhill to harbour of Porz Hir • Follow road behind beach • CA past car-park • Turn R onto path by picnic table and follow around headland • CA to road and bear R towards cottages • divert L onto path parallel with road to cottages • Level with cottages bear L under trees and CA to path TJ

Diversion: turn R to explore Pointe du Château (good sea views)

3. Turn L, follow between rocks and bear R along top of shingle beach • Bear R through stone gate-posts • Follow defined path across heathland area (at top, viewing platform on right - first glimpse of the famous house between the rocks) • **CA down towards car-park but bear R on path before car-park • CA to Maison du Littoral** (*centre d'interprétation*) **on right • CA to road**

Diversion: turn R • At end of road CA on broader path onto headland • At end bear R to the *gouffre* (a chasm across the rocky headland with the waves pounding through far below) • Returning, bear R to take a longer path back to the road

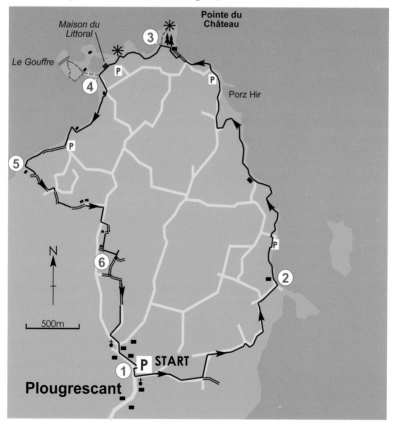

4. Turn L • At barrier bear R on larger road • 70m turn R onto path immediately beyond house • CA on path along back of beach (ignore tracks to left) • At house on right, follow R down left side of house • CA around headland to car-park • By seat turn R onto track • Follow around bay and CA up green path onto headland and turn L towards house

5. CA on path inland to left of house • CA on track • At road turn L • 75m, just before road forks, turn R onto grassy track • Follow to field entrance ahead and turn L on path • CA up track • At houses bear R on road • At TJ turn R • 175m turn L • Follow rough road R and CA to end • Turn L onto path (at the time of writing this path appeared to be infrequently used; if it's a problem return to main road and continue another 230m to the next turning left and CA on track past house to join the other end of problem path)

6. 125m at path/track TJ turn L • 100m at path TJ turn R to track and follow R • At TJ turn L and follow R (the church on the horizon is in Plougrescant) • As track becomes road CA • At church bear L • Bear R at end of church, ignoring road on L • CA past bars and cafés on left • Follow down to Place de la Mairie

Le Gouffre

OTHER WALKS in the area:

Plougrescant There are many walking routes across this peninsula which can combine with the coast path to give a longer circuit around the Pointe du Château.

PLACES OF INTEREST nearby:

Plougrescant Chapel of St-Gonery. The lead encased spire was added to the late 12th century tower in 1612. Although it buckled under its own weight it was stabilised and looks set to remain like this for a few more centuries. Inside is a 15th/16th century painted ceiling and the relics of St-Gonery. His pardon is on the last Sunday in July.

Keralio (4kms SW) Château de Keralio - late 15th century tower remains from the original *château fort*, otherwise 17th and 18th century. Exterior visitable April to October.

WALK 18: Plésidy

Length 10½ kms	Time 3 hrs	Level 2/3

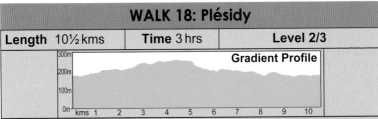

Location & parking: Plésidy, 12kms S of Guingamp via the D767 and D5. From Plésidy centre take road to Bourbriac; 1km W from Plésidy take D5 left to St-Nicolas-du-Pelem, then first road on right and park immediately.

Refreshments: bar/tabac/restaurant in Plésidy. None on route.

This is the Breton *argoat* at its best: lush green fields, deep wooded valleys, majestic and mysterious menhirs, and that whiff of nostalgia that comes from walking old railway lines.

DIRECTIONS

1. CA down the road to old water tower on right The water tower and the alignment of the small house to the right confirm that you are on an old railway. In fact it's the same metre gauge line encountered in Walk No.27, St-Nicolas-du-Pelem. The section from Guingamp to Plésidy was opened in 1923 and that from Plésidy to St-Nicolas-du-Pelem in 1924. The whole line was closed in 1938, unable to compete with improved road transport.

• **CA on road to left of water tower** • **Follow 500m to junction, bear L** • **250m turn L onto track** • **Follow to hamlet of Trévelost, turn L at cross-roads** • **At curved TJ turn R onto grassy footpath** (ignore grassy track into field) • **CA** (former railway) **into wood** (where the rough granite chippings of the trackbed are still visible) • **At bank across line of railway, turn L up grassy track** • **100m follow R**

**between fields • At road turn R
• 100m turn L onto grassy track
• 70m turn L to wood-fenced
enclosure around menhir**

The Menhir de Kailouan stands
7.4m above ground but it is
often listed as 11 metres - its
probable total size. There is a
legend that it separates the
graves of a Gallic chief and a
Roman general: that may be so
but certainly its original purpose
is lost in the mists of the neolithic.

**2. Return to road and turn L
• 650m at TJ turn R • At right
bend turn L onto track** (away
from farm) • **Follow R and CA**
The top of the rise is the highest

Menhir de Kailouan

point in Plésidy at 264m. Good views: Plésidy church spire on right,
between two hills, and Bourbriac church ahead slightly left. This is
also the watershed between the English Channel and the Atlantic
• **Just over summit turn L onto path • 300m follow L • 100m follow R
and down into wood** (Toul du - the black hole) • **Follow path**

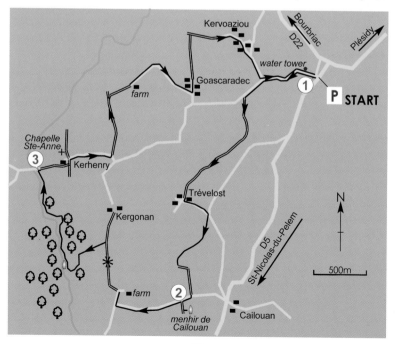

Menhir du Toul Du

steeply down - just as it levels out find menhir by stream on L The menhir du Toul Du was lost in the undergrowth until a few years ago, when the site was cleared by a small army of volunteers.

• **Return to path and CA 1km down valley** (passing a *chaos*, after which the path broadens and runs level, then descends into old leet)

3. At road turn R uphill • CA on track, follow over hill by farm • At track TJ turn L 20m to road

Diversion: CA 100m to see chapelle Ste-Anne

Main route: **turn R and follow road • 375m turn L onto track** (before the road junction visible ahead) • **500m follow R and down to farm • CA on road 700m to TJ by houses and turn L** (Goascaradec) • **CA on road to end of hamlet** (butterfly sanctuary on right) **then CA on track**

The association Vive Armor Nature has encouraged families to provide butterfly sanctuaries by leaving an area of their garden uncultivated and not using chemicals. There is now a network of such sites and local authorities have also joined in. (See http://pagesperso-orange.fr/vivarmor)

• **At far end of field turn R at track TJ • CA towards houses • CA on road into hamlet** (Kervoaziou) **and bear R • Bear R again at junction • CA** (ignore road from L) • **250m at TJ turn L and retrace route back to start**

OTHER WALKS in the area:

St-Adrien (5kms N) From the *bourg* a 'figure-of-eight' walk of 8kms reaches the R. Trieux.

St-Houarneau (10kms W) From the chapel of St-Hervé, a 7km circuit of the countryside.

Kerpert (10kms S) The 9km *Circuit des Fontaines* starts from the *bourg*. (See *Central Brittany Coast to Coast*, walk No.3)

PLACES OF INTEREST nearby:

Bourbriac (5kms W) The church has a 11th/12th century crypt, originally housing the tomb of St-Briac but now the 16th century Chapel of the Lords of Kerias dedicated to St-Lawrence.

WALK 19: St-Martin-des-Prés

Length 9 kms	Time 3 hrs	Level 2

Location & parking:	
St-Martin-des-Prés, 15kms S of Quintin on the D53 between Corlay and Uzel. Park by church.	

Refreshments: in St-Martin-des-Prés. None on route.

Pont de Kerigan

This walk provides an opportunity to visit the Étang de Bosméléac as it borders most of the southern side of the lake, a favourite fishing spot for both humans and birds. There are also options to see three chapels and in the first few kilometres there are some splendid distant views to the north.

DIRECTIONS

1. **From parking on south side of church, go east to junction and turn L** (D63 to La Harmoye and Quintin) • **50m turn R and CA on track** • **Follow R between fields to road, turn L on road** • **300m at TJ, CA on track** • **Follow R, at fork bear R** • **At road follow L** • **At TJ bear R** • **CA up past Kerguétu** (ignoring roads to right) • **At top turn sharp L** • **550m at right bend turn L on track** • **Follow R and down, then L and R to CA along right edge of field** • **At bottom of field CA on track 50m to road**

2. **Turn R and CA 700m, follow to junction and turn L** • **Follow L** (ignoring road on right) • **Just short of entrance to car-park on**

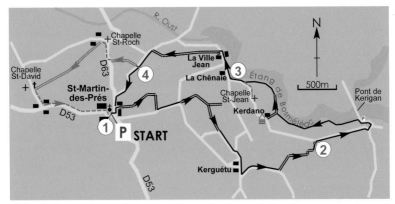

right, take path L • **CA on path under trees following near edge of lake** (Étang de Bosméléac) The *étang*, was created by a barrage on the river Oust at Bosméléac (not on route), to feed the Rigole d'Hilvern and the Nantes-Brest Canal • **At field follow right edge** • **At track (from Kerdano) follow R (still following edge of lake)** • **At end CA on path** (look left for spire of chapel of St-Jean) **to road**

Diversion: turn L to see chapel and its *fontaine* a few hundred metres further on at Kerdano. The chapel is dedicated to St-John the Baptist and is the result of the successive visions of a child in 1817. The position of the *fontaine* relates to the site of an earlier chapel. Return and CA to point No.**3**)

Main route: **bear R along road**

3. At junction turn R • CA through La Chênaie • Ignore road left (short-cut back to St-Martin), **CA to hamlet of La Ville Jean • At two tracks on left, take second • Follow 950m to road and turn L**

- **Pass road right, CA to grassy track on right**

4. Diversion (additional 2¼ kms): turn R onto grassy track • Follow 400m to road, turn R • At chapel St-Roch fork L

St-Roch (1340-1378) came from Montpellier and probably trained as a doctor. Having

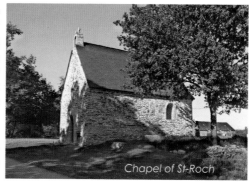
Chapel of St-Roch

cared for victims of bubonic plagues he eventually fell ill himself and in order not to infect others he retired to the forest, where a dog brought him daily a loaf of bread stolen from its master's table. The latter, intrigued by the dog's behaviour, followed it and, discovering the saint, was able to help him. St-Roch is always depicted with a dog, hence the French expression 'as inseparable as St-Roch and his dog'. Naturally, St-Roch is invoked for protection against rabies, plague and epidemics.

• Take first track on L • CA 1150m to road by cross (bear right and cross road to see chapel of St-David if desired) • Turn L • 250m at TJ turn L • Follow road back into St-Martin, bearing R towards church

4. Main route: **CA on road • At junction with D63, turn left and follow D63 into St-Martin**

OTHER WALKS in the area:

Barrage de Bosméléac (5kms E) A 5km circuit of the eastern end of the Étang de Bosméléac, includes the barrage and a short diversion to the start of the Rigole d'Hilvern. It connects with this walk at the Pont de Kerigan.

St-Gilles-Vieux-Marché (10kms S) *Circuit des gorges de Poulancre*, 8kms. Park in Place du Bourg and head for the *salle polyvalente*. A wide variety of countryside from lakes to rocky crests.

PLACES OF INTEREST nearby:

Cartravers (2½kms N on D63) an enormous double lime kiln on the right of the road.

71

WALK 20: Plouha - Plage Bonaparte to Beg Hastel

Length 8 kms	Time 2½ hrs	Level 3

Location & parking:
2kms from Plouha on the
D786 towards Paimpol,
turn right, following signs to
Plage Bonaparte. Large car-park at end of road.

Gradient Profile

Refreshments: in Plouha. None on route.

Beg Hastel and La Mauve

This walk starts from the historic Plage Bonaparte and having climbed the cliff follows the coast path inland. It soon leaves it to explore the villages that nestle between Plouha and the sea, arriving at the coast again behind the spectacular headland of Beg Hastel ('Castle Head' in Breton) and its two islands, Le Pommier (the apple tree) and La Mauve. The coast path is then followed all the way back to Plage Bonaparte.

Plage Bonaparte is the WWII code name for what was formerly known as the Anse (bay) de Cochat. The beach (today accessed through a tunnel constructed in 1973) was the final embarcation point for allied air crew rescued from all over France, lodged, fed and guided to this point by the Resistance organisation *'Réseau Shelburn'* (the Shelburn network). Between January and August 1944, 142 allied aviators and secret agents made the trip. Gathered at nearby Kerlévénez at the home of Jean Gicquel they waited for the code message *'bonjour tout le monde à la maison d'Alphonse'* to tell them a MGB would be waiting in the bay. The Resistance would then guide them through the minefields and down the cliff to the beach at low tide on a moonless night, where they waited up to their waists in water to be picked up by boats and ferried out to the MGB under the noses of the Germans in their cliff-top blockhouse. Incredibly, this operation was repeated eight times without being discovered, although the Germans were in the end suspicious of the 'Maison d'Alphonse' and burnt it down. There is a monument by the upper car-park and many plaques around the tunnel expressing gratitude and appreciation of the local people who risked not only their own lives but those of their families if they were discovered.

DIRECTIONS

1. Facing sea, take path up cliff on R • At top bear L through car-park to coast path descending right of monument • Follow inland to road and follow road L • At right bend ignore coast path going left on no-through-road, follow road R into Tevros • At junction go L • CA over cross-roads • At right bend CA on smaller road

2. At TJ follow L • 275m at right bend CA on path into wood • Cross stream • Fork L • Cross end of road and CA on grassy path left of house • CA on earth track between fields • At road go L 80m to end of stone wall on right, go R on track • 400m at road turn L • In Kersalic CA at first junction, follow road R

3. Diversion: at second junction CA 300m to TJ, turn R and follow road to chapel at La Trinité. This chapel is mentioned as early as 1354. The stone beside the road nearby has a dished top and is said to be an offering stone dating from the Iron Age, c.500BC. To return, partially retrace route but CA on road towards Beg Hastel.

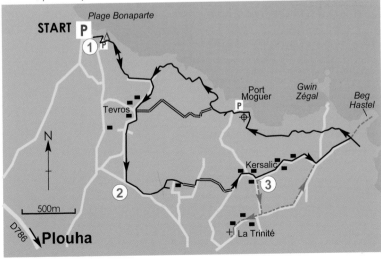

3. Main route: **at second junction go L and CA through Kersalic • At TJ turn L then fork R • At end of road CA to coast path**

Diversion: CA on path through bushes to walk out along Beg Hastel

Main route: **turn L to follow coast path • 300m at road go L 30m then R again on path • Follow coast path** (looking back, observe the anchorage at Gwin Zégal - one of the last remaining post anchorages made by planting trees in the sand) • **CA** passing large sea-mark **down to Port Moguer • Cross road to CA on coast path bearing L up opposite cliff • 75m fork R • almost at top, ignore broad track from left** (from Tevros) **• CA on coast path • Just after Plage Bonaparte comes in sight, follow path L to road • Follow to junction, turn R and retrace outward route**

Gwin Zégal

OTHER WALKS in the area:

Plage Bonaparte As an alternative beginning to this walk, the cliff path on the left from the car-park has a branch inland to the Chapelle St-Samson (15th century). Turn L here to the junction (maison d'Alphonse and stele) then CA for 1.3km to point No.2 of this walk.

Gwin Zégal (see map) The *Sentier des Falaises* climbs from the port and goes south to the Pointe de Plouha, the highest cliffs in Brittany at 104 metres.

Lanvollon (7kms SW) A collection of 11 walks in the Lanvollon/Plouha area is available from local TOs.

PLACES OF INTEREST nearby:

Kermaria (5kms W on D21) The chapel is 13th century and in addition to the interesting porch with a room above for records and a balcony for delivering judgements, there is a magnificent 15th century fresco of the Dance of Death.

Lanleff (10kms W) The 'Temple' is a circular, arched structure, once thought to be Roman. Later opinion puts it at 11th century and based on the Church of the Holy Sepulchre in Jerusalem.

WALK 21: Hillion

Length 8 kms	Time 2½ hrs	Level 3

Location & parking: Hillion, 5½ kms north of the N12 near Yffiniac (just east of St-Brieuc). In Hillion centre, park by the *Foyer Rural* / Espace Palente.

Gradient Profile

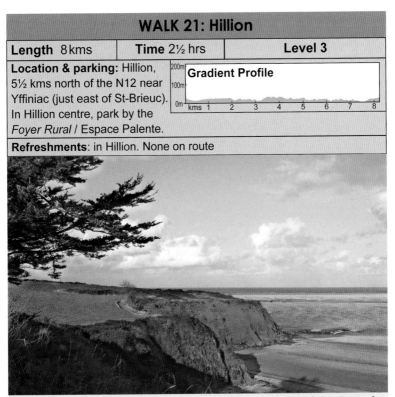

Refreshments: in Hillion. None on route

Hillion is on a peninsula projecting into the centre of the Bay of St-Brieuc, along the eastern side of the Anse d'Yffiniac, where the tide recedes by several kilometres. Binoculars are essential equipment on this walk: the views are distant and there is plenty to see - birds particularly. The Bay of St-Brieuc is a winter migration site for 1.7 million water birds. Depending on the season, one can hope to spot Brent geese, shelduck, curlew, spoonbill, red shank, green shank, oyster catchers, avocet, turnstones, silver plover, ringed plover, sanderlings, knot, dunlin and godwit. Even osprey and sea eagles are not unknown. For more information take the diversion to the *Maison de la Baie*.

DIRECTIONS

1. From car-park exit turn R on road • CA on main road 500m (following R fork at 350m) • At town exit sign, turn R • 50m at end of road CA on footpath • CA on stony track • At road turn L • At end of road bear R on stony track (views to right across Anse de Morieux to Chapelle St-Maurice on its little hill) **• At road turn R • Just before campsite/mobile home park, take earth path on L • CA on this coast path**

2. At Plage de Lermot (swimming opportunity) **descend to road, turn L 30m then sharp R to car-park • CA through picnic area • 800m climb steps to path TJ, turn R to Pointe des Guettes** (orientation table, views of both Anse de Morieux and Baie de St-Brieuc) • **CA on coast path round other side of point • Descend towards inlet, cross concrete steps and CA on coast path to Pointe du Grouin • CA 1km and descend to St-Guimont beach**

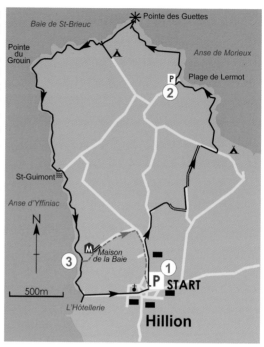

(*lavoir* and *fontaine* on right, behind beach) • **Cross road, up steps and CA 900m to stone seat and path arriving from left**

3. Diversion: turn L, 100m to *Maison de la Baie* on left *Eco-musée* and study centre with information on birds and wild-life in the Bay of St-Brieuc • **Either** return to coast path and continue, **or** (short-cut) CA inland on road, turn R at junction and CA to regain Hillion centre

In the Baie de St-Brieuc mussels are cultivated on oak posts, known as 'buchots'. In the spring, mussel larvae attach themselves to ropes strung between the posts. The ropes are then wound around the posts and the mussels left to grow, being harvested 18 months later.

3. Main route: **CA on coast path • At L'Hôtellerie join road along front and CA onto beach to see cliffs** (the strata of the alluvial cliffs illustrate the climatic changes over the last 350,000 years - puts our pre-occupation with global warming into perspective) **• Return to road and follow inland to Hillion centre, bearing L ahead from church to car-park**

Typical low tide activity in the Anse d'Yffiniac

Anse d'Yffiniac

OTHER WALKS in the area:

Morieux (5kms E) From the centre of the *bourg* a circuit of 10kms explores the country to the NW. It can be prolonged to 15kms by a loop to the SE of the *bourg*, before returning to the start.

Langueux (5kms SW, on opposite side of Anse d'Yffiniac) A 13km circuit from the Place François Mitterand includes almost 3kms of coast path.

Coëtmieux (6kms SE) A circuit of 8½kms, or 5½ via a short-cut, goes from the centre of the *bourg* to follow the river Gouëssant. Plenty of interest for naturalists.

PLACES OF INTEREST nearby:

Morieux (5kms E) The church dates from the 11th century and includes frescoes, discovered in 1995 and now restored.

Bout de Ville (Langueux, 5kms SW) The '*Briquetterie*' is a museum of life a century ago based on a former brick and tile factory. Nearby, is a restored section of narrow gauge railway with rolling stock and locomotives.

WALK 22: Laurenan

Length 10½ kms	Time 2¾ hrs	Level 2

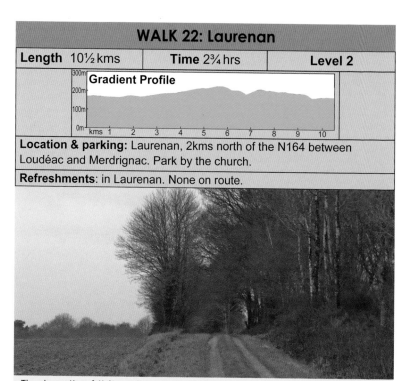

Location & parking: Laurenan, 2kms north of the N164 between Loudéac and Merdrignac. Park by the church.

Refreshments: in Laurenan. None on route.

The length of this walk puts it at the limit of the medium category but it presents no difficulties and the going is good, at first on a former railway then across country on well-made farm tracks and returning along the footpath following an old Roman road.

The stone cross on the grass between the car-park and the church is 12th-13th century.

DIRECTIONS

1. From church car-park, return to mini-roundabout and turn R
• 650m in Le Châbre turn L • 50m turn R along old railway track-bed (soon passing old station on right) This was the metre gauge line from Carhaix to St-Méen-Le-Grand, part of the Réseau Breton. One of the last sections to open, it operated from August 1907 until closure in 1967. The station building is now a private house.
• 700m CA over track by road on right **• CA 1km**

2. Diversion (2.5km) to Chapelle St-Yves at Tertignon: turn R on rough road • At TJ turn R • CA to cross and chapel on right (They say that this chapel benefited from a gift from Louis XIII and his queen, Anne d'Autriche, in thanks to God for their son, the future Louis XIV, *le Dieudonné*) • Return up road but CA at junction to rejoin track-bed further on

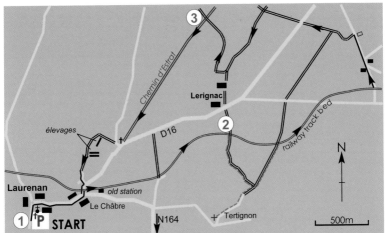

2. Main route: **CA on track-bed • 550m CA over rough road** (diversion rejoins) **• 650m CA over another road • 650m at road turn L** away from track-bed • 200m on left - note old bread oven **• CA past two roads on right • Just past farm on right** (abandoned, but note how the walls are constructed of layers of compacted earth, *terre à banchage*, with footings and corners in stone), **turn L on track • 100m follow R • 200m CA**, don't follow track left **• At road, cross and CA on track • Over hill at track crossroads, turn L • 800m, just short of farm** (Lerignac), **turn R down into valley • At bottom follow R • CA 700m to track crossroads at top of hill**

3. Turn L and CA on old Roman road (Chemin de l'Estrat - the straight road - the Roman road from Corseul, *Fanum Martis*, to Vannes, *Darioritum*) **• CA** in a straight line **1.6km to road** (D16) **• CA on road 50m** (La Croix du Chêne Dubé on right) **turn R • Fork L immediately on track • Past *élevage*, follow L • CA past another *élevage* • At road CA • At fork go L • At TJ turn R and CA over track-bed to retrace outward route**

OTHER WALKS in the area:

Laurenan A longer version of the present walk (12kms) continues on the railway for a further 2 intersections, there striking north to the chapel of St-Lambert and returning by the Roman road.

Goméné (5kms SE) A 6km circuit from the *bourg* to find three mysterious crosses at le Tertre Feuillet.

Plémet (7kms W) From Vaublanc, a circuit of 11kms including an old iron foundry.

PLACES OF INTEREST nearby:

La Chèze (15kms SW) Ruins of a 12th century château (see 'Central Brittany Coast to Coast' by Penny Allen).

WALK 23: Plédéliac - Château de la Hunaudaye

Length 7½ kms	Time 2 hrs	Level 2

Location & parking:
St-Ésprit-des-Bois, 2½ kms east
of Plédéliac on the D55.
Park in centre opposite garage.

Gradient Profile

200m
100m
0m
kms 1   2   3   4   5   6   7

Refreshments: in St-Ésprit, at Le Chêne au Loup, and crêperie near château in season.

Unlike so many villages that are not the centre of their *commune*, St-Ésprit-des-Bois has retained some life. It has a baker, a bar/restaurant and even a service garage. Right in the centre of the village, the Ferme d'Antan (Farm of Yesteryear) re-creates the life of a typical farm at the beginning of the 20th century, open to visitors in season. The highlight of this walk, however, is the Château de la Hunaudaye, which comes suddenly into view as you go over the brow of a hill.

DIRECTIONS

1. **Walk uphill away from chapel, cross D55 and CA on road opposite** • **At TJ and track opposite** (with cross under oak trees, picnic area) **turn R on road** • **At 6-way junction** (Le Chêne au Loup) **CA on 3rd road right** (signed Le Clos Chantoux), **soon becoming track** • **At left bend CA on grassy path** • **CA down** *chemin creux* • **CA across track and down another** *chemin creux* • **By water pumping station bear L up road** (Manoir de Bélouze on left, dating from 15th century, originally the home of a captain serving at the castle, now a *ferme auberge*) • **Ignore roads left, then right, CA to crossroads**

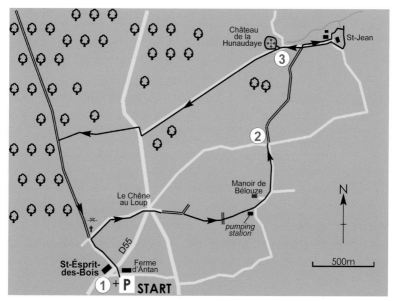

2. At crossroads CA on rough road (Château de la Hunaudaye soon visible ahead) • **800m at TJ turn R** • **200m at TJ in village, turn L** • **CA to turn R in front of bread oven, then bear L down into woods** • **At bottom bear R up onto bank** • **CA over stream to path TJ and turn R** • **CA up to road and turn R back into village** • **Turn L at junction to retrace route**

St-Jean is the oldest village in Plédéliac. Before the castle was built, St-Jean was called La Ville de la Hunaudaye. It once held fairs, and must have benefited from the proximity of the château.

• Pass road on left • CA to TJ before château (Either visit château - open in season - or walk round outside of moat)

The Château de la Hunaudaye dates from 1220, when Olivier Tournemine obtained permission to construct a castle to oversee

Château de la Hunaudaye

the River Arguenon (2kms E), a natural defensive feature which Pierre de Dreux, Duke of Brittany at that time, was developing by flooding the river valley to create a string of lakes (hence Jugon-les-Lacs). During the War of Succession (1341-64), the Tournemines being allied to the Penthièvres, the château was attacked and destroyed by the Montforts, supported by the English. Pierre Tournemine, the only surviving male heir, began reconstruction in 1467, on the plan of five towers joined by curtain walls. It was completed in 1474. The *domaine* de la Hunaudaye was raised to a barony in 1487 and the Tournemines became important at the Duke's court. The château escaped damage in the Wars of Religion (1592-98), both sides having agreed upon its neutrality. In 1783 it was sold to the Marquis de Talhouët. In 1793 the Republican administration in Lamballe had decided to dismantle the Château de la Hunaudaye to prevent it being used by the Chouans, but a group of revolutionaries from Lamballe took it upon themselves to perform this task, burning the lodgings, destroying the roofs and floors and partially demolishing the curtain wall. Thereafter the castle quietly deteriorated. It was listed as a Historic Monument in 1922 and was bought by the state in 1930, to ensure its conservation. A recent programme of restoration has retained the atmosphere of a medieval ruin, whilst improving its facilities. It is open for guided visits and groups.

3. From château entrance, turn R and follow road 1km to TJ, there turn R • 50m turn L onto straight track, becoming footpath • 600m at TJ with track, turn L • Follow track to cross under oak tree passed on outward route and CA on road into St-Ésprit

OTHER WALKS in the area:

St-Ésprit-des-Bois A 12km circuit departs from the present circuit near Bélouze, follows the river Arguenon southwards and returns to St-Ésprit via the cross and picnic area at the start of this walk.

Plédéliac (2kms W of St-Ésprit) A 15km circuit in the forest of La Hunaudaye. Joined with the present walk, it makes about 20kms.

Trégomar (5kms W) A 14½km circuit through varied countryside and including a menhir.

Jugon-les-Lacs (7kms SE) From the *bourg*, a 19km circuit goes southwards around the Étang de Jugon, and a 8km circuit to the north takes in various points of heritage interest. From Dolo, 2km S of Jugon, a 9km circuit visits country and lake-side, including a *manoir*.

PLACES OF INTEREST nearby:

St-Ésprit-des-Bois *Eco-musée de la Ferme d'Antan*, peasant life at the turn of the 20th century. Open April to September.

WALK 24: Guenroc

Length 9 kms	Time 3 hrs	Level 4

Location & parking:
Guenroc 3½ kms east of
D766 Dinan to Caulnes:
turn off at La Croix
Guessant or follow signs from Caulnes.
Down main street from church, find car-park on left, in Rue du Courtil.

Gradient Profile
200m / 100m / 0m kms 1 2 3 4 5 6 7 8 9

Refreshments: possibly in Guenroc. None on route.

The name Guenroc (white rock) derives from an outcrop of quartz on the hill behind the church. This beautiful natural feature has been rather over-run by Christian symbolism, but the village is also known for its unusual chimneys. The nearby barrage of Rophémel on the river Rance has created a long lake with abundant bird-life. Its beautiful scenery is explored on this walk.

DIRECTIONS

1. **CA down Rue du Courtil • At crossroads CA • Follow L, fork R and CA 400m to end of road • Bear R through car-park • CA on footpath along side of valley • At path TJ go L, shortly after, fork R on upper path • CA and follow down towards water, across stream valley and up other side • At path TJ go L, then follow sharp L • zig-zag down and shortly after zig-zag up again** (this pattern is often repeated until the route leaves the lakeside, about 3kms ahead) • **CA past viewpoint and seat** (opposite a second flooded valley) • **CA upwards, eventually arriving at a track • Follow track L**

2. **Short-cut:** 100m follow track R and CA to road • Turn L and follow road 600m • At left junction, return route is footpath on R

2. Main route: **bear L off track and CA on footpath • Follow L down**

to water and CA along side of valley • CA past jetty (left) and shelter • Shortly after, ignore smaller path left, CA up main path • CA 1km to viewpoint on left and picnic area on right

Short-cut: turn R through picnic area and follow path to road, turning R to La Rosais

Main route: **CA leaving picnic area on right • Follow down across stream and climb on other side • Cross another stream higher up, bear L • At track follow L but at L bend CA • At corner of field CA on track along L edge of field** (away from lake at last) • **Follow L, then R between fields to road • Turn R on road, CA 300m**

3. **Diversion:** ignore road R and CA • At next junction see La Croix des Defas, marking border between bishoprics of Dol and St-Malo as well as plague cemetery of 1638-9 • Then either CA on road all the way to Guenroc or return to previous junction

3. Main route: **turn R • Follow 1km to La Rosais • Almost at top of hill turn sharp R • At road end bear R** (pond on left) • **CA along R field edge, then between hedgerows • Emerge to CA along L field edge • At road follow R • 100m at junction, turn L on footpath along L field edge • Bear R at corner and follow to left of ditch • Bear L between posts into** *chemin creux* (Chemin creux de Bédée, thought to be over 2000 years old) if flooded, take to the field edge • **At road turn L • Ignore right turn to La Ville Fleury, CA bearing R through Le Cariou** (house on right has the best chimneys in Guenroc, and decorative corbels at the eaves) • **At junction bear L ahead • At next junction bear R ahead • 50m turn R to car-park**

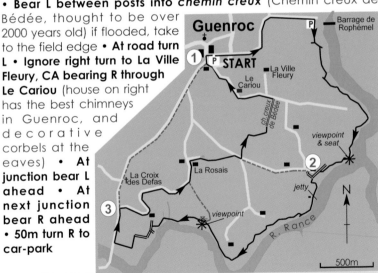

OTHER WALKS in the area:

Yvignac-la-Tour (9kms NW) A short walk (4kms) but with a rich architectural heritage and pleasant countryside.

PLACES OF INTEREST nearby:

Bécherel (10kms E) Just over the border in Ille-et-Vilaine but worth a visit for its bookshops (it's the Breton Hay-on-Wye) and a celtic stele with a relief carving of a fertility god.

WALK 25: Tonquédec

Length 11 kms	Time 4 hrs	Level 3

Location & parking: Château de Tonquédec. From the D11 Lannion to Plouaret take the D30 eastwards, then the D31 to Tonquédec. From the church follow signs to the Château de Tonquédec. Park at the château.

Refreshments: crêperie at Château de Kergrist, otherwise Tonquédec village.

This is a favourite walk, starting and finishing at a spectacular medieval castle but also taking in two chapels, a *fontaine*, three mills in picturesque settings, a stately home and its gardens (visitable in season) and the incredibly beautiful River Léguer. There are several possible combinations of short-cuts and diversions (see map) so one doesn't need to do the whole circuit to see most of its features. Timing the walk to finish at the Château de Tonquédec when it's open provides the perfect ending to an enjoyable outing.

The first castle at Tonquédec was built of wood on the promontory overlooking the R. Léguer. It was superceded by a stone castle in the mid 12th century, but this was destroyed on the orders of duke Jean IV in 1395 after its owner, Rolland III de Coëtman, had supported the revolt of Olivier de Clisson. It was rebuilt in the early 15th century. In the Wars of Religion Tonquédec and the neighbouring castle at Coat Frec (4kms N) were held for the protestant king Henry IV. The notorious catholic adventurer Guy Eder de la Fontenelle captured Coat Frec while the garrison were away defending Guingamp, but he was later captured in 1593 and held prisoner in the tower at Tonquédec until ransomed. The château last saw action in 1614, when it was occupied by the

85

brother of the vicomte de Tonquédec with a handful of soldiers in support of the duc de Vendôme, then governor of Brittany but disloyal to the regent Marie de Médici. The latter ordered the people of Lannion to take up arms. A raiding party scaled the tower at night and entered through the roof to surprise the sleeping garrison, who quickly surrendered. Afterwards, the town of Lannion asked that the castle be rendered militarily unserviceable and in 1626 Cardinal Richelieu was happy to give the order for its battlements to be dismantled. Militarily useless and inconvenient as a residence the château was then abandoned.

In 1880 the Château de Tonquédec was acquired by the de Rougé family, who are descended from Prigent, vicomte de Tonquédec, the builder of the first stone château. The de Rougés still own Tonquédec today.

DIRECTIONS

1. **From Château de Tonquédec walk a few metres back up road towards Tonquédec • 30m beyond information hut take path R up under trees • Follow L • At road, cross to CA on path • Bear R to join path from right, follow L • At track go R, past house • At road go L • Follow R then L at junction • 300m turn R** (signed Pen ar Guer) **CA on track to right of house • 200m CA on grassy track past farm • 300m take path L down into woods** (ignore broader path ahead) **• Cross stream at bottom and CA • At house on right CA on path • At top, bear R and CA on track past houses on left • At road bear R, follow to left of cross and CA 120m to end of road**

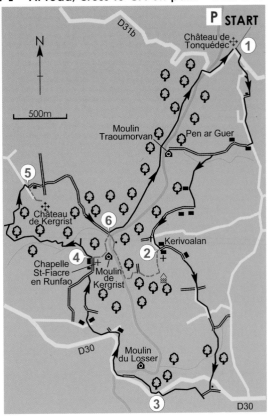

86

2. Short-cut: turn R 100m to chapel on L (Chapelle N-D de Kerivoalan) • CA from chapel into wood 50m • At two successive path forks bear L • Follow L and down to right bend (Diversion 1: here bear L off path to descend to Fontaine de Kerivoalan, then return to path)

• Follow R and CA at bottom • Bear R to path junction and turn L downhill • At river Léguer turn R and follow bank • At little house bear L to footbridge • Cross to point No.**6**

(Diversion 2: here turn L to Moulin de Kergrist and from there, if desired, follow path up hillside on right to Chapelle St-Fiacre-en-Runfao and nearby manor house - point No.**4**. Then either return directly to point No.**6** or follow main route through point No.**5** to point No.**6**.)

(Diversion 3: from point No.**6** CA up track to Château de Kergrist. At top, at secondary track into château grounds, CA right of farmhouse to road. Turn left here to château entrance and crêperie. Gardens open to public in season.)

2. Diversion: follow short-cut (above) as far as chapel (and *fontaine* if desired) then return

2. Main route: **turn L on track, follow bearing R of last house** • **CA on footpath** • **At end, CA on road** (ignoring tracks right and left) • **Follow 250m to crossroads** • **CA 120m** • **At left bend take track on R** • **20m bear L on path** • **CA into woods, follow down across stream and CA up side valley** (path tends to left side of this valley) • **At road** (D30, busy) **cross and CA on path** • **Just past house on left** (many tracks and field entrances here) **take first track on R** • **At path TJ go R** • **Follow L and CA down sunken path**

3. At road (D30 again) **follow L** • **At right bend bear R onto path down into woods** • **Just short of mill** (to right ahead) **turn R to field, follow left edge 10m to corner and CA** • **Follow track ahead up to road** • **Follow D30 R over bridge, then 400m up to left bend** • **Take path bearing R towards house** • **Follow L to cross side-road to track** (but do not follow)• **CA on path next to main road** • **50m follow R up sunken path** • **At houses, cross little road and CA past right end of hedge** • **Turn R and CA on path away from houses** • **At track TJ bear L** • **At stony track bear R** • **Follow to chapel** The Chapelle St-Fiacre-en-Runfao,

15th-18th century, is part of the estate of the Château de Kergrist (see point No.5). It contains the tomb of Guezno de Penanster, who was 'chef de la Chouannerie' in north Morbihan before emigrating to England in 1802. He returned to France in 1814. The chapel has been recently restored by the Château de Kergrist's current owner, M. Huon de Penanster.

4. Short-cut: turn R down far side of chapel • Follow path down into valley by Moulin de Kergrist • CA, bearing R to footbridge over river Léguer (do not cross) at point No.**6**

4. Main route: turn L down far side of old manor house • Bear R onto path • Follow down into woods • **At fork bear L • Cross stream and CA up other side** (muddy) • **Follow twisting path up into pine wood • 500m at path TJ bear R • At field follow L edge • Follow edge R and CA under trees • At another field follow L edge** (Château de Kergrist comes into view on right) • **At corner of field CA on wide grassy path along R edge of another field • 25m bear R through gap in hedge to road • Turn R towards Château de Kergrist**

Diversion: (in season) CA to crêperie/reception to visit château and/or its gardens

5. 30m bear L onto track • At house on right CA on grassy track • At secondary track leading to château, cross over to track opposite and follow it 900m down to river Léguer

6. Turn L on path following river downstream • Follow almost 2km to road • Turn R over bridge and follow road 400m up to Château de Tonquédec

OTHER WALKS in the area:

Tonquédec Also starting from the château, a circuit of 8kms descends the right bank of the R. Léguer to cross at the Moulin de Kerguiniou and return via the chapel at Kerfons.

Cavan (5kms E) An 11km circuit explores a broad sweep of countryside back towards Tonquédec.

Ploubezre (8kms N) An 11km circuit starts from the chapel at Kerfons, swings NW towards Ploubezre, crosses the R. Léguer at the chapel of St-Thècle (see Walk No.2) and returns via Kermeur.

PLACES OF INTEREST nearby:

Château de Tonquédec (on route) Medieval castle.
www.chateau-Tonquédec.com
For times of opening consult Lannion TO, or see
www.ot-lannion.fr/Parcs--jardins-&-chateaux.html .

Château de Kergrist (on route) 15th to 19th century residence, furnished and inhabited by the owners. Renowned gardens.
http://kergrist.monsite.wanadoo.fr

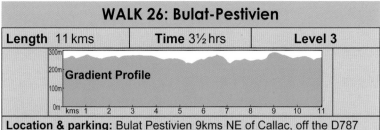

WALK 26: Bulat-Pestivien

Length 11 kms	Time 3½ hrs	Level 3

Gradient Profile

300m 200m 100m 0m
kms 1 2 3 4 5 6 7 8 9 10 11

Location & parking: Bulat Pestivien 9kms NE of Callac, off the D787 Callac to Guingamp. Park in centre.

Refreshments: in Bulat Pestivien. None on route.

This is a long country walk deep in the heart of central Brittany. The landscape varies from seemingly impenetrable marshy woods, through open farmland and the gorse and heather covered '*landes*' or moorland. Almost everywhere there are enormous granite boulders, though unfortunately some of those nearer the path have been defaced by information panels intended to enhance your walking experience. The occasional villages have retained some solid 18th century houses and the *bourg* of Bulat Pestivien is rightly proud of its architectural heritage. The richly carved 16th century church has the highest spire in the department (66 metres), although, surprisingly, this is a late 19th century addition. The *pardon* is on the second Sunday in September and the following day, Monday, the vast open area in front of the church is the scene of the annual horse fair which attracts thousands of visitors. The Maison du Granit on the opposite side of the square has an information point and occasional exhibitions.

DIRECTIONS

1. From gateway of churchyard, turn R and go through square to road • Bear R on road and follow to roundabout

Diversion: (500m) CA to Fontaine du Coq on L, then CA to Fontaine des Sept Saints on R • Return to roundabout

Main route: **at roundabout turn L** (D31 to St-Servais) • **Just before summit turn L • Follow round into Lannouzec • CA to TJ, turn R • CA on track • 150m turn L at TJ • Follow 300m • Just before track ends in field, bear L onto path • CA, bear L through bank, then bear R to CA** (path very muddy until raised onto bank across bog through wood) • **CA across stream, up bank and turn L • 150m turn R onto sunken path • 200m turn R onto wider sunken path, follow to hamlet** (Goarem Guellec)

2. Past first barn on R, turn L on track • 75m fork L (ahead) • Follow L, then R and bear L on grassy path • 100m Follow L • Follow down 200m turn R • Follow over bank to join sunken footpath with field on L • At corner of that field climb steps up bank on R • Follow L edge of field • At corner continue around L edge of field • CA through gap in hedge and CA on path • At track turn L and follow 500m to road

3. Turn L 500m • Where track crosses road go R on track • Follow L, ignore track on R, follow down to Kerjulou • CA through village centre to road, turn R • Follow road 200m, turn L onto track • Follow to big rocks • Follow track R past 1st rock, then turn L on path, bearing R then L over bank • Follow R edge of field 200m to corner, go through field edge and turn L • 40m follow R •100m along top edge of wood, follow into sunken path • Follow L down zig-zag path, bearing R towards bottom and CA • Bear L onto track • Follow to road at Goascaër

4. Turn L • At fork go R uphill • 450m at cross turn L onto track

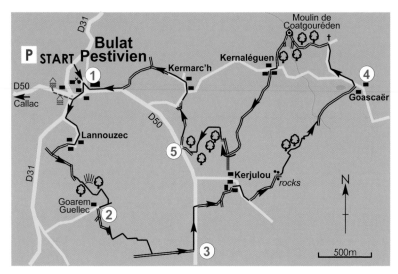

After 200m at a left bend, a landscaped valley on the right leads up to the site of the 14th century *manoir* of Coatgoureden. It was in ruins at the beginning of the 19th century.

Moulin de Coatgoureden

• **Follow down to mill** (Moulin de Coatgoureden, now a private house) • **Follow track round in front of mill and CA** • **Bear R uphill and follow 300m to road** • **Turn R into** (deserted) **hamlet of Kernaléguen** • **Opposite house, turn L onto track** • **Follow 900m** • **At L bend, take track sharp R** • **Follow 150m, turn L up into woods** • **30m follow R on woodland path** • **Exit wood, turn L along L edge of field** • **At top corner, bear L over bank, bear R on other side to CA** • **10m CA over bank** • **Follow L 20m, then R** • **Over another bank CA down through woods bearing L on grassy path** • **At track turn R and follow to D50**

5. **Turn R, then immediately R onto grassy track** • **Follow alternate track and path to road** • **Turn R to Kermarc'h** • **At fork bear L** • **100m fork L** • **At end of road CA on track** • **Follow L** (Circuit des Tailleurs des Pierres leaves R here) • **CA to D50 and follow R to centre of Bulat Pestivien**

OTHER WALKS in the area:

Bulat Pestivien A 3.5km circuit named 'Circuit des Tailleurs des Pierres' (stonemasons' circuit) starts at the church and takes a route to the NW of the bourg. It can be incorporated into the end of this walk.

For a 9.5km circuit incorporating the 'Tailleurs des Pierres' and part of this route see *Central Brittany Coast to Coast* Walk No.5.

Maël Pestivien (5kms SE) A 13km circuit explores country to the south, including 'la Chaire des Druides'.

PLACES OF INTEREST nearby:

Manoir de Bodilio (3.5kms N) 17th century manor, now a museum of manors. Open April to October, Saturday & Sunday afternoons. Exterior visits all year.

La Chêne de Tronjoly (3.5kms N) 1000-year-old oak tree. Follow signs from D31. Any day except Sunday.

WALK 27: St-Nicolas-du-Pelem

Length 13 kms	Time 3½ - 4 hrs	Level 2

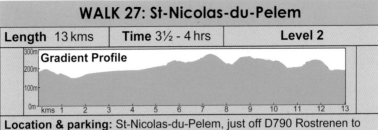

Location & parking: St-Nicolas-du-Pelem, just off D790 Rostrenen to St-Brieuc. Park in Place du Kreisker, near church and TO.

Refreshments: in St-Nicolas-du-Pelem. None on route.

Until 1836 the chief town of this *commune* was Bothoa, which had been a parish since medieval times. It included the Château de Pelem (1622) and the Chapelle St-Nicolas. Since then St-Nicolas-du-Pelem has developed instead of Bothoa. The present day church, formerly the Chapelle St-Nicolas, dates from the 15th century and was extensively restored in the 19th. This walk sets off westwards and turns north up the valley of the Ruisseau de Faoudel, along a former railway track - easy walking in quiet, wooded scenery - followed by a trek over high ground and valleys to Bothoa, returning to St-Nicolas by way of the Étang de Beaucours.

DIRECTIONS

1. **From west door of church walk uphill through Place du Kreisker and CA on Rue de Boisboissel** (post office on right, *mairie* on left) **• At roundabout CA • Follow 1km to crossroads at bottom • CA towards swimming pool • At TJ turn R • CA to Moulin des Rochers** (mill of the rocks) **• CA on track 2kms to road** This track is the old railway line from St-Nicolas-du-Pelem to Plésidy, then on to Guingamp, opened in 1924 and closed in 1938. After crossing two bridges note the remains of a mill on the left, Moulin du Bois.

2. Cross road and CA on same track (narrowing at times to a footpath, not having been converted to a 'voie verte' - yet) **1.3kms to former mill on R** (Moulin de St-André, now a small farm) • **CA on road to TJ • Turn R, cross river and follow road up to St-André** • **Just <u>before</u> cross, turn L onto track • 500m at left bend, CA on sunken path • Emerge onto track and CA to road • Turn L up road 150m • Just over summit, turn R onto track • At end CA down path** (hamlet of Kerbastard to left) • **Join road bearing R, follow down and up to TJ • Turn R and follow road 500m to Bothoa**

Bothoa today is noted for its school museum, recreating a village school of the 1930s.

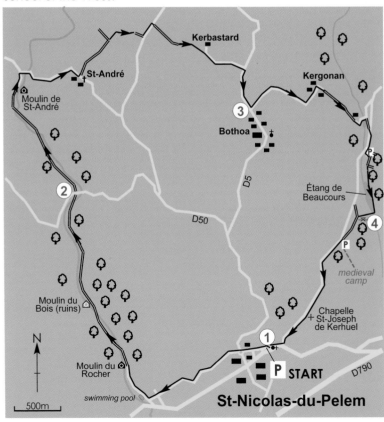

3. Do not enter village but turn L to Kergonan • CA on road 1km • In Kergonan, follow road R and CA on track • Follow down to house on left and CA on road • Hairpin L to head of small lake • CA to other side and turn R on track • At road bear R and follow down 200m • By forest sign turn L through car-park to track going R (ignore track ahead uphill) • **Where path bends left uphill, CA on smaller path on level** • **70m CA along left side of Étang de Beaucours to barrage**

Chapelle St-Joseph de Kerhuel

4. Turn R over barrage • CA uphill (100m picnic table on left) • CA uphill, bearing L • At pole barrier CA (ignore track from right) • CA parallel with road, eventually joining it at car-park

Diversion: bear L from car-park, following signs to medieval camp, 800m, and return

Main route: **join road and follow 1km to TJ** passing disused (actually a restored ruin) Chapelle St-Joseph de Kerhuel (1669)on left • **Turn R into St-Nicolas-du-Pelem, bearing R towards church**

Before reaching the church, look between houses on the right to see some crenellated ramparts on the hillside. This was to have been a château, begun in 1875 by the Comte de Boisboissel to welcome his relative, the Comte de Chambord, pretender to the French throne. In fact the Comte de Chambord had effectively given up pretending in 1873 when Maréchal Mac-Mahon established the 3rd Republic and consequently this château was never completed.

OTHER WALKS in the area:

St-Antoine (9kms NW) See Walk No.3, Gorges de Toul-Goulic

Kerpert (10kms N) The 9km *Circuit des Fontaines* starts from the *bourg*. (See *Central Brittany Coast to Coast*, walk No.3)

PLACES OF INTEREST nearby:

Bothoa (see map) Musée Rural de l'Éducation. www.musee-ecole-bothoa.blogspot.com

Le Ruellou (1km S) Late 15th century chapel with 18th/19th century extension. Noted for its hand-operated bell wheel with a peel of 12 bells.

WALK 28: Gouarec to Bon Repos

Length 12½ kms	Time 3½ hrs	Level 3

Gradient Profile

Location & parking: Gouarec, on the N164 between Rostrenen and Mur-de-Bretagne. Park by former station, now the TO and *gîte d'étape*.
Refreshments: in Gouarec and Bon Repos.

Abbey of Bon Repos

A walk of two halves, the outward journey is more strenuous, climbing to the Landes de Liscuis and culminating at two neolithic alley graves. There follows a sharp descent to the track-bed of the former Réseau Breton railway, then down to the abbey of Bon Repos, an ideal place to take a break before tackling the easier second part of the walk, following a quiet woodland path and then the canal towpath back to Gouarec.

NB: a new, more northerly route for the N164, by-passing Gouarec and the valley of the Blavet is due to open during 2009. The N164 referred to in these directions and map is the old route.

DIRECTIONS

1. **From TO cross main road bearing R, away from town • Fork L to Rosquelfen** (rue de Stang ar Goff) • **375m** (50m before junction) **turn R up steps to footpath • CA 125m, follow L and CA 250m, past** *fontaine* **&** *lavoir* **to road • Turn R and follow road to TJ • Turn L then R immediately • CA 250m to crossroads, turn R and follow down • At R bend with gated track L, CA on path • CA over stream • 50m at path TJ turn R • Follow down towards picnic area on N164**

2. **Just short of picnic area, turn sharp L, through barrier to path climbing • Follow up to summit of Landes de Liscuis and CA • Follow 3km, through old slate workings, into wood, past ruined**

quarry buildings and CA to first alley-grave on Left • At path junction here turn R • Pass another alley grave on R, CA to path crossroads at Point No.3

Remains of quarryman's shelter

Alternative: at first alley-grave, turn L to see another on left, then continue to path TJ and turn R to rejoin main route at Point No.3

Or: wander at will to see all three alley graves

The alley graves are neolithic, dating between 3000 and 1500BC

3. Alternative: (2kms added) CA and follow path around above gorge • Descend to D44 and turn R • Bear R onto track before viaduct and follow to point No.4.

3. Main route: **turn R downhill** (views of Gorges du Daoulas to left) • **400m at right bend in birch wood, take little path L, descending steeply** (beware loose slates) • **Ignore path from left, CA down to former railway and bridge** In September 1967 the last train passed along this section of the metre gauge Réseau Breton from Carhaix to Loudéac. Wherever feasible, the former track-bed has progressively been re-opened as a *voie verte* (green way).

4. Do not cross bridge, turn R on track and follow 400m to road • Turn L, follow down to N164 • Cross and turn L to go over bridge over river Daoulas • Bear R immediately to cross picnic area, CA on road, cross bridge over R. Blavet/ Nantes-Brest Canal

Alternative: follow towpath to point No.5.

Main route: **bear R onto grassy track to R of bar/café • CA on**

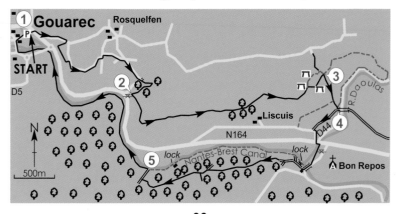

96

track into woods •100m fork L • 100m fork R • CA almost 1km to pass track from right, then path from left • Follow path ahead 800m to track, turn sharp R • Follow down to canal

The Nantes-Brest Canal

5. Turn L along towpath • Follow 2.8kms to join road in Gouarec, by bridge • Turn R over bridge • CA 150m on road (across second bridge) • Turn R and CA to start

Take a few moments to explore this part of Gouarec with its granite houses, including the Pavilion des Rohan, built in 1634 as a hunting lodge for the dukes of Rohan. It now houses the HQ of the AIKB, an association for integration in central Brittany.

OTHER WALKS in the area:

Bon Repos (see map) A shorter circuit to see the alley graves and Gorges du Daoulas follows paths described above, in whichever direction preferred. (see *Walking Brittany* by Judy Smith, Walk No.13)

Rosquelfen (see map) An alternative circuit incorporating the alley graves and the Landes de Liscuis uses the quiet road that runs to the north, parallel with the outward path of this described route. If desired, it can be extended into a figure-of-8

Gouarec A waymarked circuit in the Bois de Gouarec starts from the TO

Caurel (13kms E from Gouarec) An 8km circuit of the woods beside Lac de Guerlédan.

PLACES OF INTEREST nearby:

Abbey of Bon Repos (on route) Founded by Alain III de Rohan in the 12th century, a Cistercian abbey that survived until the Revolution. The buildings are gradually being restored by an association.

Les Forges des Salles (2kms SW of Bon Repos) An 18th century ironworking village in the Forêt de Quénécan. Open afternoons in season.

WALK 29: Kermoroc'h

Length 13½ kms	Time 4 hrs	Level 3

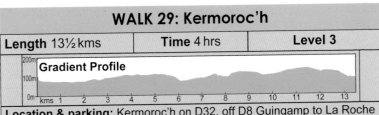

Location & parking: Kermoroc'h on D32, off D8 Guingamp to La Roche Derrien. Continue on D32 through Kermoroc'h to bottom of hill, park on right, entrance marked by totem-pole.

Refreshments: in Kermoroc'h. None on route.

This walk is based on three parallel valleys; that of the Ruisseau du Poirier, the river Jaudy and the Théoulas ruisseau and combines a good stretch of each with some pleasant cross country walking. There is plenty of interesting flora and fauna to look out for, as well as a medieval hospital or leper colony and the nearby *commanderie* of the Order of St-John of Jerusalem.

DIRECTIONS

1. **From car-park CA on footpath** (following the stream for 2kms, mostly on the right bank but crossing and re-crossing once. There are children's play areas and information panels in French about the wildlife. Some trees are named with descriptive panels in French, although tree names are also given in Breton and English. About half way there is a 19th century chapel to the left of the path • **At road turn L** • **60m fork L** • **In Kerrohan fork R** • **60m turn R**

98

onto track • 75m turn L onto path • Follow down into valley and CA up other side • At track follow L • At road at top go R on road • At TJ turn sharp L • CA on road 1km, passing right turn to La Chavraie, taking next right turn onto track (signed 'Listember')

2. At track fork go R • Follow 500m to TJ, turn L onto road • Follow to D20, cross and CA on path • Follow R 200m to field • Follow left edge of field, then bear R to gorse thicket and follow path through • CA on path through trees (see photo page 98) • At road turn L • 300m (just before TJ) take path R • Follow down to road • Bear R 30m, then bear L on track • Follow down across stream and bear L along *chemin creux* • 75m bear L onto path

3. Follow path (upstream) alongside R. Jaudy • Just beyond waterfalls path bears L • Follow up into trees, bear L and R over ditch and CA (through wood of beech and chestnut) • CA over bank and through hazel thicket • Eventually, path rejoins river

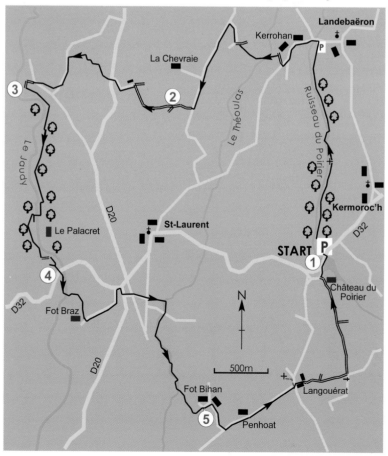

• **Follow up onto bank and turn R along it • 50m pass barricade, ignore path right and CA 100m to footbridge**

The hamlet ahead is Le Palacret, a former *commanderie* of the Order of St-John of Jerusalem. More recently the mill has been used in the processing of flax to produce linen, one of Brittany's traditional industries. At the time of writing, Le Palacret was being restored and converted to an eco-museum on the 'Linen Road' and an environmental resource centre with accommodation and a restaurant.

• **Cross footbridge and climb bank • Ignore waymarked path left along river, but CA uphill, bearing L • Follow path back to river then away again 80m to turn L on track down to picnic tables • CA past picnic tables • At path TJ bear L to D32**

4. Cross D32 and CA along river Jaudy at edge of meadows • At corner of field, cross river by old stone bridge • Bear L up *chemin creux*

Old stone bridge over the Jaudy

Wall around leper colony at Fot Braz

Note old stone wall on right - this encircles Fot Braz, the old leper colony belonging to the *commanderie* at Le Palacret. The occasional hole in the wall at table top level is indicative of the medieval view of leprosy which was considered highly contagious. Lepers were isolated from the outside world in semi-monastic agricultural colonies where they were said to be going through Purgatory on Earth, or between life and death. Matthew Paris writing in the early 12th century estimated there were 19,000 leper colonies across Europe.

• **At top bear R • CA up and follow path alongside wall • At road turn sharp L • Follow L to TJ with D32, turn R • 50m turn R again • 100m turn L • Cross another road and CA 140m to TJ • Cross and CA to follow path down into valley • Cross stream and turn R • Follow path up stream • At road, cross and CA on path following stream • Cross bridge and bear L under fallen tree-trunk • Follow path upstream, crossing and re-crossing the stream, for 700m • Cross for last time and follow path ahead uphill • CA to road**

5. **Bear R and follow up to TJ • Go R and follow 250m to TJ • Turn L and follow road 750m through Penhoat to Langouérat**

Diversion: at TJ turn L on road 100m to ruined chapel of St-Louis of Langouérat, and return.

Main route: **at TJ bear L and CA along side of building opposite, then bear R on track • CA ignoring track left • At road by cross, turn L on track • CA** (ignoring track right) **800m to farm -** called Château du Poirier - there are traces of old walls and a moat, whereas the even earlier Château du Poirier, the feudal *motte* on the hill half a mile away, was built only of wood, surrounded by two deep circular ditches • **Bear L up to road and turn R • CA 100m to D32, bear R 100m, then L into car-park**

OTHER WALKS in the area:

Kermoroc'h (starting from the same car-park as this walk, where an information panel maps the routes) A short (4.4kms) walk to the feudal *motte* of the old château du Poirier (not the farm at the end of this walk). Also, a medium walk (10.8kms) incorporating a large part of this walk.

Prat (10kms NW) A 13km figure-of-8 walk starts from the car-park by the Étang de Poulloguer, just southeast of the *bourg* on the D74. The route passes the Chapelle St-Jean at Trévoazan, one of the chapels founded by the *commanderie* of Le Palacret.

PLACES OF INTEREST nearby:

Bégard (7kms W) Armoripark for children's activities, swimming etc.

WALK 30: Paimpol

Length 15½ kms	Time 5 hrs	Level 3 (4 on coast)

Gradient Profile

200m
100m
0m
kms 1 2 3 4 5 6 7 8 9 10 11 12 13 14 15

Location & parking: Abbaye de Beauport, Kerity, on D786 towards Plouha, 2kms from Paimpol. Park in abbey car-park.

Refreshments: in Kerity and in Kerfot.

By the Étang de Danet

A long walk but it divides nicely into three parts with plenty of opportunity to take short-cuts and leave sections out as required. The largest part is through the woods (Bois de Beauport) following the river Corré up to Kerfot, returning on higher ground but still mostly under trees to the beautiful Étang de Danet. From here it's a short way back to the start but the full walk continues through a bit more wood to Le Vieux Bourg and Ste-Barbe, joining the coast path at Boulgueff for a roller-coaster with many steps back to the Abbaye de Beauport. Allow for a full day to take in the abbey as well, then visit the lively harbour and town of Paimpol in the evening.

The Abbaye de Beauport was founded in 1202 by Alain de Goëlo, comte de Penthièvre. Almost 20 years earlier he had founded the monastery of St-Rion on the nearby Île des Cerfs, but its island location proved an obstacle to managing its lands, both here and in England. The monastery failed to prosper and Alain transferred its rights and possessions to a new foundation on the mainland. For the Abbaye de Beauport he chose Augustinian canons, the

Abbaye de Beauport

Prémontrés from the abbey of La Lucerne in Normandy. ('Prémontrés' because their founding saint, Norbert de Xantien, had been shown, *prémontré*, in a vision where to build a monastery). The new abbey grew rich and powerful under medieval feudalism, but times changed, particularly with the introduction of the *commende* in 1516 whereby abbots became lay appointees of the king and often acted for their own profit. By this and other erosions of the abbey's economic base, decadence and poverty gradually set in. In 1651 the *abbé général* of the Prémontrés took the matter in hand and a vast restoration and rebuilding project was undertaken. It is mostly the buildings of this period that are seen today. In the 18th century the canons took to a more worldly existence, becoming involved in politics and even at first supporting the Revolution. It overtook them in the end and they were forced to leave in 1790. The abbey became the property of the state and was used as a saltpetre factory. In 1797 it was sold off and was subsequently used partly as a farm and partly by the local community of Kerity to house the *mairie* and the community school. It was listed as a historic monument in 1862. In 1992 it was bought by the Conservatoire du Littoral and there is an on-going programme of restoration.

DIRECTIONS

1. **From car-park return to road and follow R** • **50m turn L, ignore no-through-road on left, CA into open area** (former camping) • **Bear L and CA on footpath** • **At end of clearing on right, bear R, cross stream then bear L on first track** • **300m bear L and recross by bridge, bear R over bank and CA following stream** • **250m bear L and climb to CA up valley at higher level** • **250m bear L to road** • **Cross road and CA on track** • **At road, cross bearing R and CA on path snaking through wood** • **Follow into valley, turning L at bottom and follow stream to multiple path junction**

2. **Bear R over river Corré** (footbridge) • **CA 50m, fork R** • **250m ignore '*propriété privé*' notice** (walkers are allowed) **and CA on path following river Corré** • **250m bear R** (path joining from left) **and CA to left of Corré** (do not cross) • **500m bear L to join another**

path, follow **R** • **250m ignore bridge R** (steps on other side lead up to an artificial lake) • **At next footbridge cross and bear L across small field, bearing R to CA on path up log steps** • **At path junction bear R** (ignore bridge left) • **Ignore another bridge left and CA up into park** • **At games area turn L and follow path to road** Take a tour around church at Kerfot. It was re-built in 1922, but the bell-tower and south porch are 16th century. In the crypt is a *fontaine* at the entrance to an underground passage.

3. Turn L and follow path to left of bank (through picnic area) • **CA beside road** • **Ignore steps left** On the high ground on the opposite side of the road is Correc, where once there was a *château*, the seat of Alain de Goëlo, comte de Penthièvre, founder of Beauport Abbey • **At right bend, turn L by car-park and follow path through woods, climbing R** • **CA on path, ignoring others right and left** • **At road, follow it L** • **325m at TJ CA on track** • **At right bend, go L on path** (following what must once have been a wide road marked by banks either side) • **At track TJ turn R** • **At road follow it L** • **At TJ CA on footpath** • **Follow down to multiple path junction** (arriving at the fork passed earlier)

2. Re-cross footbridge and bear R and sharp R to CA on path through woods • **CA over stream** (bridge) **up steps and bear R on path** • **At lake on right** (bird-life) **CA to path junction at far end**

Short-cut: CA to reach D786 near abbey (800m)

Main route: **turn R across barrage to road** • **Turn L 50m to footpath on R** • **Follow up between gardens** • **At road turn L** • **Follow to end, CA on track 50m then turn L on footpath** • **Follow down and past lakes on left** • **At path junction bear L across two streams and bear R on other side of valley** • **CA** (ignore path left) **and cross stream** • **CA to emerge from woods and CA on grassy track** • **At track junction follow stony track L** • **At road follow it R** • **At TJ turn L and follow to main road**

4. Cross D786 and CA on Rue du Vieux Bourg • **Follow R** • **At TJ go R then L immediately** • **CA, left of chapel Ste-Barbe, to cross-roads**

Short-cut: CA on road to coast path at Pointe de Kerarzic

Main route: **turn R** • **300m turn L to *table d'orientation*** (100m) **then return to road** • **CA to right bend, bear L on track** • **Ignore track on left, CA down to coast, bearing R to large car-park**

5. At far left corner of car-park CA on coast path • **1.2km at road turn R downhill** • **At entrance to oyster farm turn L onto coast path** • **Within sight of abbey, bear R down to broader path, follow R and down steps** • **Bear R and L across stone bridge and CA on causeway** Before restoration in 1995 the sea defences had fallen into disrepair, endangering the abbey buildings. The St-Brieuc to Paimpol railway followed the old 18th century dike until the 1950s,

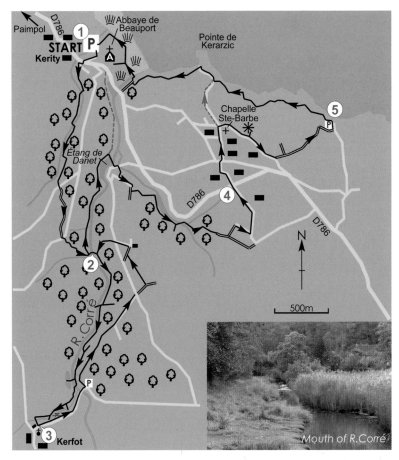

Mouth of R.Corré

after which it was not maintained • **At path junction go R** (to right of abbey) • **Past abbey turn L on path to right of walled gardens** • **At far corner of wall, turn L, through arch, bear R to car-park**

OTHER WALKS in the area:

Lancerf (9kms W) There are various possible walks in the forest of Penhoat-Lancerf overlooking the river Trieux. Start from the Maison du Littoral at Traou Nez (see *Walking Brittany* - Walk No.15).

PLACES OF INTEREST nearby:

Paimpol and its harbour. The Musée de la Mer (open April - Sept), in a former cod drying factory on the west side of the harbour mouth, tells the story of the Icelandic cod fishing industry of the late 19th, early 20th century.

There is also a costume museum open in July and August only.

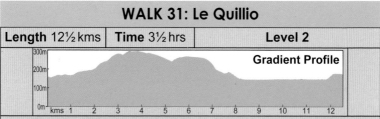

WALK 31: Le Quillio

Length 12½ kms	Time 3½ hrs	Level 2

Gradient Profile

Location & parking: Le Quillio, 9.5 kms NE of Mur-de-Bretagne on the D35 to Uzel. Park opposite *mairie*.

Refreshments: none on route.

Rigole d'Hilvern

This walk has many themes: the Breton linen cloth trade, vernacular and religious architecture, pre-history and the Nantes-Brest Canal. There is of course a connection between the linen cloth trade and the vernacular and religious architecture: it was the wealth from linen that enabled the merchants to contribute generously to the construction of richly embellished churches and chapels in the 16th and 17th centuries, and finance their grand houses in the 18th century. Pre-history is found at the highest point of the parish, the site de Lorette (298m). And the Nantes-Brest Canal? Well, much of the return route is along the Rigole d'Hilvern, a 63km feeder for the canal.

Before starting the walk, take a little time to look at Le Quillio - the church with its *enclos paroissal* and just up the road opposite the church (but facing away from it, on the right) a large house showing the distinctive architectural style typical of 18th century cloth merchants' houses in this area.

DIRECTIONS

1. **Facing *mairie*, take road on L towards D35 • Do not join D35 but bear L onto road opposite *lavoir*** (originally a *doué*, a linen bleaching tank lined with slate, but little of this can be seen) **• Follow 500m round to D35 • Turn L , follow D35 for 400m • Fork R**

up D69 • 100m fork R • 150m at right bend turn L onto stony track • **Follow 1km** (shortly, a pleasant view looking back to Le Quillio) ignore tracks right and left • **At road cross to inspect Fontaine de N-D de Lorette** (the water is said to be good for ear-ache), **otherwise turn R 50m**, then R up road to Chapelle N-D de Lorette

Le Quillio church

The original chapel on this site was probably built toward the end of the 14th century by the Comte d'Uzel in fulfilment of a vow. It fell into disrepair and was replaced by the present building (which is often open) in 1854. The nearby cromlech of 28 stones, white quartz on the north side, dark schist on the south, is the remains of a late neolithic burial mound.

2. Leave by track to L of cromlech (the track straight ahead takes a longer route with unnecessary descent and climb - see map) • **Follow 570m to track TJ, turn L** • **400m at road turn R** • **Follow 750m**

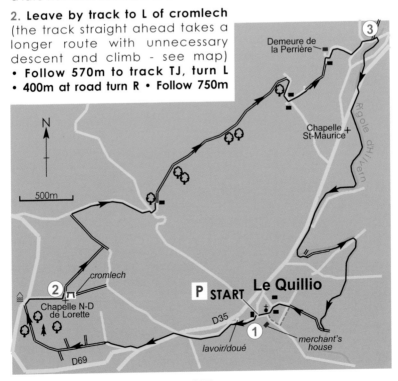

to TJ, turn R • 50m turn L • CA
on track past house • CA
1.75km (track follows a ridge,
partly in woods partly by fields:
good distant views either side)
• **Descend to TJ and turn R**
• **Follow road down through S-
bend • At houses turn L • At left
bend into farm, CA on track
• At houses CA on road • At TJ
on bend by Demeure de la**

Perrière (cloth merchant's house, 1736) **turn R down road • Follow
down to TJ, turn L • 150m at TJ turn R • CA 100m to Rigole d'Hilvern**

Hilvern is a hamlet by the Nantes-Brest Canal near St-Gonnery. The
Rigole d'Hilvern (1836) carried water from the upper reaches of
the R. Oust at Bosméléac (north from here, see Walk No.19) to the
canal's highest point (192m) east of Pontivy. From here it fed flights
of locks in each direction. It is currently undergoing restoration by
a local association.

3. **Turn R along left bank of Rigole • At road CA along left bank
• At main road (D35) cross and CA on R bank • Passing very close
to D35, cross minor road and CA on right bank of Rigole • Follow
Rigole L away from D35,** over tributary from right • **50m ignore
bridge, take track R, still following Rigole's right bank • Cross minor
road and CA • Cross another minor road and CA • At track over
Rigole turn sharp R away from Rigole • Follow L uphill between
fields • CA to road**

Alternative: (to see merchant's house, if missed at beginning of
walk): turn sharp L and CA to TJ. Turn R and follow 200m down to
church, passing merchant's house on L

Main route: **CA on road opposite, bearing L towards church • CA
past church and follow down to** *mairie*

OTHER WALKS in the area:

Le Quillio A 9km walk to St-Thélo, outwards along the Rigole
d'Hilvern (starting from the point where this walk leaves it) to
Le Rest, then by road to St-Thélo; returning via roads and a
different (more westerly) section of the Rigole.

St-Caradec (7.5km S) A 15km circuit taking in La Chapelle
St-Laurent, then using sections of the Rigole d'Hilvern to reach
Hémonstoir to the south.

PLACES OF INTEREST nearby:

St-Thélo (3kms SW) *La Maison des Toiles*. Museum of the linen
trade actually housed in the Manoir Boscher Delangle, the oldest
of the houses once belonging to prosperous linen merchants.

WALK 32: Plaine Haute

Length 13 kms	Time 4 hrs	Level 3

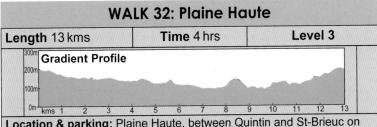

Gradient Profile

Location & parking: Plaine Haute, between Quintin and St-Brieuc on the D40. Park by the *mairie*.

Refreshments: in Plaine Haute and in Ste-Anne-du-Houlin.

Moulin de St-Méen

As its name suggests, Plaine Haute is on a high plain of rather featureless farmland but nearby is the scenic valley of the river Gouët, where this walk leads to hidden menhirs, ancient stone-slab bridges (*ponts à dalles*) ruined mills and a *chaos* of rushing water and gigantic rocks.

DIRECTIONS

1. From front of *mairie* turn R down road • 250m (just before village exit sign) **turn L • 250m** (opposite le Tertre aux Oies) **turn R on track • 125m ignore track L, CA bearing R to CA on road in La Noe • At cross-roads CA to Carblou • At road end, CA to turn R round far end of barn on right • Follow path down into valley • Cross stream and CA up other side of valley and bear L • At track, turn R to larger track and turn L • Follow 500m to road in St-Eloy**

2. At the crossroads is a Merovingian (5th-8th century AD) stone cross. There are two others of this period in Plaine Haute, at Cassière-Blaye and Carcaux • **Turn L on road • 150m turn L onto footpath between hedgerows • CA 900m to a distinct 'hump' in the path:** here divert L over bank, bear R and look for large menhir 50m away, but beware boggy ground *Le menhir de L'Hôpital* or

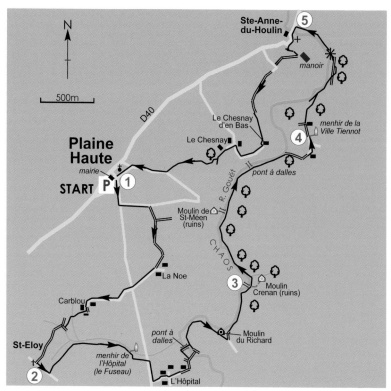

le Fuseau (the spindle) - neolithic Return same way to path • **CA to road and turn R** • **200m turn L** (signed L'Hôpital d'en Bas - former property of the Hospitallers of St-John) • **At crossroads CA** • **CA on track past farm** (left) • **Follow down L, then R** (ignore entrance ahead) • **Half-way down to ford, take footpath L** • **Follow down to bridge and cross over** • **CA to path TJ, turn L** • **Path follows river, soon reaching Moulin du Richard** • **Follow to R of mill, climbing to road** • **At road turn sharp L downhill, past mill entrance** • **CA on path following river 500m to footbridge** (do not cross)

3. Diversion: at footbridge turn R and bear L over dry leet to see ruins of Moulin Crenan • Return same way

3. Main route: CA by river, crossing tributary stream • **750m** at ruins of Moulin de St-Méen on other side of river (footbridge) **CA to R of river as before** (ignore path right) • **At stone-slab bridge do not cross, CA** • **At track and fishing hut, leave riverside path, follow track R** • **CA on road, bear L and CA on smaller road** (ignore road right)

4. Diversion: at top of hill where road ends (but continues as track) divert R on path 70m to see Menhir de la Ville Tiennot, and return

Main route: **follow track to house entrance on right and CA on footpath** • **Bear R down to river** • **CA following river as before, shortly climbing to go to right of** *chemin creux* • **Follow path through wood, rejoining** *chemin creux* **further on** • **50m bear L downwards to view-point above weir** • **CA to road**

5. Turn L on road and cross bridge to Ste-Anne-du-Houlin (café) • **CA past chapel** (originally founded by and belonged to the lords of the manor of La Ville Daniel) • **At far end of crash barrier on right bend, take path L** • **Follow sharp L and CA uphill** • **At manor, turn sharp R onto track and CA** *Le manoir de la Ville-Daniel* (1559), built by the Le Voyer family, who also founded the chapel in St-Anne-du-Houlin. The arms of the Le Voyer family are still on the fortified tower of the manor house, as well as in the chapel. The manor's lands including the chapel were confiscated at the revolution • **At TJ turn L and follow R** • **At road end CA on track** • **CA down into valley and up other side** • **At track end bear R to CA on narrow** *chemin creux* • **Follow down to Le Chesnay d'en Bas and follow R** • **At entrance, turn R onto road** • **Follow R to Le Chesnay, turn L** • **Before house entrance ahead, bear L on track** • **50m** (in trees) **fork R, then follow L** • **CA 500m to road, turn R and follow up into Plaine Haute** • **At cross-roads CA** • **150m cross zebra-crossing to** *mairie* **car-park**

OTHER WALKS in the area:

Plaine Haute There are a number of possible circuits and combinations that can be followed around Plaine Haute and the neighbouring *communes* of Plaintel and St-Julien. Details from local TOs or *mairies*.

Boquého (14kms NW) Starting at a *calvaire* 1.5kms SW of the *bourg* (direction St-Fiacre), an 8km circuit visits four more crosses and offers a diversion to a menhir.

PLACES OF INTEREST nearby:

Péran (6kms ENE, near where D10 crosses D700) A 10th century Viking camp in a remarkable state of preservation (marked as 'Anc. Camp Romain' on IGN map).

WALK 33: Bréhand

Length 15 kms	Time 4 hrs	Level 3

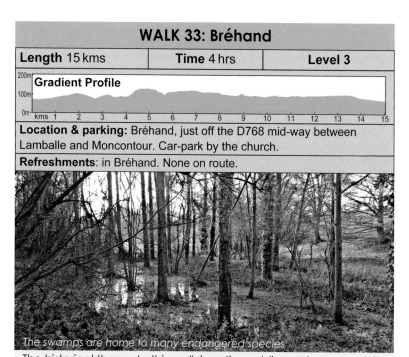

Gradient Profile

Location & parking: Bréhand, just off the D768 mid-way between Lamballe and Moncontour. Car-park by the church.

Refreshments: in Bréhand. None on route.

The swamps are home to many endangered species

The historical theme to this walk is anti-republican chouan activity in the early 1790s. The countryside was in revolt against the Republic's conscription of 300,000 men in 1793 to counter the first European coalition against France. Local insurgents sought their leaders among those with some military experience; around Bréhand it was a former officer of marines, Amateur-Jérôme-Sylvestre de Bras de Forge de Boishardy, who proved to be a popular and charismatic leader, earning the nick-name 'le Sorcier' (the wizard). He quickly became the general commanding all Chouans in Côtes d'Armor. In March 1795 he negotiated a truce with the republican General Hoche, but it was not respected and hostilities resumed. In June 1795 Boishardy was caught and killed by republican soldiers near the Chapelle St-Malo on the road to Moncontour, but his legend lives on in Bréhand, his home town.

DIRECTIONS

1. **From car-park go to right side of church, bear L to war memorial and CA on Rue de Mené** (Salle Alain Glâtre on left - this was formerly the *auditoire*, the place where, before the Revolution, the lord of Launay dispensed justice) • **50m fork L** (on D80) • **350m fork R** • **CA past orchard and Manoir La Ville Louët on left** (The residence of Joséphine de Kercadio, 'fiancée' of Boishardy, where forged assignats, Republican paper money, were found) • **Beyond buildings turn R on track** • **At road turn L** • **350m at**

crossroads turn L • 800m cross river and turn R on minor road (signed Moulin Hesry) • **Bear L of house and CA on track** • 250m turn R into field and follow L edge • **Follow edge R and CA down into valley** • At stream follow path L • **CA up valley** (passing areas of swamp which are sites of scientific interest harbouring many endangered species) • **Join wider track and CA**

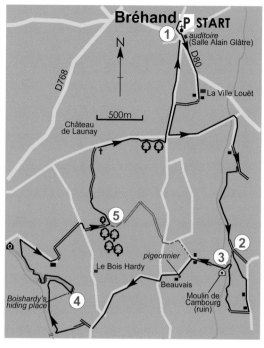

2. At multiple junction (two paths leaving right)

Short-cut (easy): take first path R and follow to wooden bridge over stream (on main route)

Main route: **take second path R • CA uphill • Bear L to road and turn R • 350m at hill-top turn R on track • 200m follow R and CA down into wood • Bear R then L to stream • Cross side stream and follow main stream down valley to wooden bridge** (short-cut rejoins)

3. Cross and bear R to follow path left up hillside (on left are the ruins of the Moulin de Cambourg, abandoned in 1919) • **At top CA to join track • At houses CA on road to junction**

Short-cut: fork R • At TJ turn L • At TJ turn R and L immediately • 450m follow sharp L • At end bear R into field and follow L edge to wood, bear R 50m and enter wood to reach point No.5.

Main route: **fork L • At farm follow road R** This farm is on the site of the Manoir de Beauvais. The *pigeonnier* remains to the left of the junction and one of the barns incorporates the vault of the private chapel. The house was destroyed in the 18th century to provide materials for restoring the family's Château de Launay (passed, but not seen, later on this walk) • **At TJ turn L and immediately R** • **CA 800m to cross-roads** (the large house and farm visible on the right is Le Bois Hardy, the Chouan general's family home) • **CA**

150m, at left bend turn R onto track • 100m fork L before pylon • At end CA on path • Follow briefly into valley (do not cross bridge), turn sharp R back up side of valley to field • Follow L field edge 600m • At far corner (do not cross bridges) bear R up narrow *chemin creux* • CA up valley to footbridge (Boishardy's hiding place in the rocks is on the right. This is only 300m from his manor house at Le Bois Hardy, across the stream)

4. Cross footbridge and bear L to return down other side of valley • At bottom cross both bridges and CA along R field edge • 100m turn R over stream and up bank • Turn L to follow L field edge • At mill pond bear R to road • Turn R on road • At farm follow L and CA 600m on track to road • Turn R • 100m turn L on track • Follow to left of main wood and into trees

5. Staying under trees, turn L on path (short-cut rejoins) and follow along L field edge • At corner CA on track • At road turn R (after 50m, remains of old cross on right, grounds of Château de Launay on left) • Follow road 500m then, just after slight right bend, take path R into woods • Follow L • At road turn L to cross-roads • CA towards Bréhand, either directly or retracing outward route

The old 'auditoire' in Bréhand

OTHER WALKS in the area:

Landéhen (5kms NE) From the *bourg*, a circuit of 13kms to the south can be shortened to 8kms, or 4kms by means of short-cuts.

PLACES OF INTEREST nearby:

Abbaye de Boquen (15kms SE) Founded by Olivier II, Comte de Dinan, in 1137 with a community of Cistercians from Bégard, it was closed at the Revolution but was revived in 1936 by Dom Alexis Presse, and is now occupied by the Sisters of Bethlehem. The restored 12th century abbey church is an Historic Monument. Open every day 9-5, except during religious services.

WALK 34: Dahouët

Length 12 kms	Time 3½ hrs	Level 3

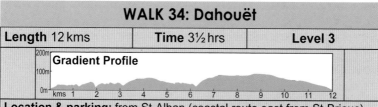

Location & parking: from St-Alban (coastal route east from St-Brieuc) take D786 to Pléneuf-Val-André, then follow signs to the port (Dahouët). Go left of harbour to large car-park.

Refreshments: in Dahouët, and Jospinet in season.

A coastal walk down the eastern side of the Bay of St-Brieuc from the fishing port and marina at Dahouët to the mussel cultivation centre of Jospinet, where there is a seafood restaurant on the harbourside in season. The route diverts inland half way but with the option of continuing on the coast path. The return route across country is peaceful and bucolic.

DIRECTIONS

1. **From car-park turn R on road towards harbour mouth • Bear L up Quai-du-Mûrier • Turn L up Chemin de la Sancie • Take 1st turning R** (at crossroads) **• 80m turn R onto track • 50m turn L onto coast path • 800m cross road** (driveway to little building on headland) **and bear R to CA on coast path • Just short of beach follow path L**

2. At Port Morvan turn L up road and immediately R on Route de la Fontenelle • 300m (before house at top on left) **turn R on coast path • At corner of field bear R uphill • Follow 1km to end of rough road and beach**

Alternative: cross road and CA on coast path to car-park at Le Cotentin (*table d'orientation* right)

Main route: **follow rough road up away from beach • At TJ turn R • 50m bear R on track • 500m at summit, ignore track right, CA on track downhill • At bottom bear L on road and CA to TJ in La Cotentin • Turn R • 200m at junction, turn R** (signed *plage* and *table d'orientation*) • **CA on road to its end at car-park** (*table d'orientation* ahead)

3. Turn L onto coast path • CA and down to road above Jospinet, turn sharp R downhill • 50m (before junction) **turn sharp L onto footpath • CA up valley • Shortly after end of oyster sheds** (right),

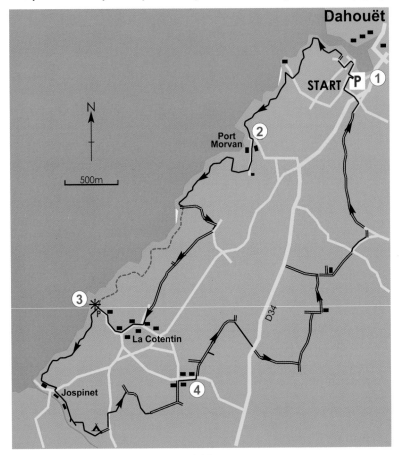

fork L • 50m turn L uphill past wooden barrier and up log steps • Through another barrier bear R along R edge of lawn below chalet park • CA on path to R of chalet park and follow L to rough road • CA to TJ with road, turn L • 130m turn R on footpath • At track follow R • CA on footpath between fields, then CA on muddy road • Bear L at track fork, CA into village • At TJ turn R

4. **150m turn L and CA on rough road** (ignoring track left and path right) • **Follow R then at left bend take path on R** • **At road** (D34) **cross and CA on track** • **At track TJ turn L** • **450m at track TJ follow R, then follow L by houses** • **350m at left bend, take track R** • **80m ignore track left, follow main track L on far side of farm** • **At road CA on road opposite** • **200m** (across valley) **take 1st track on L** • **80m at road go L and CA on track** • **Follow track 1¼ kms, becoming road at end** • **At crossroads** (just short of D34) **turn L** • **Cross over D34 and CA down road opposite** • **At TJ turn R to car-park**

Dahouët

OTHER WALKS in the area:
St-Aaron (8kms SE) From the *mairie* there is a 17km and an 11km version of a country walk, including the Manoir de Maupas, and the longer version traversing the Bois de Coron.

PLACES OF INTEREST nearby:
Bien Assis (10kms E) Château dating from the 15th century. Open from Easter to September.

WALK 35: Cap Fréhel & Fort La Latte

Length 12 kms	Time 3½ hrs	Level 2

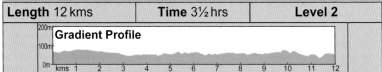

Location & parking: from the D786 between Erquy and Matignon, take the D16 to Plévenon. From Plévenon follow signs to Fort La Latte. Continue to the end of the road and park in car-park.

Refreshments: in season, at Fort La Latte and Cap Fréhel.

Cap Fréhel

Having arrived at the car-park it seems odd not to be setting out for Fort La Latte, but patience will be rewarded. This is a walk of three parts and the first is a balmy inland section across to the other side of the headland, through farmland initially but becoming increasingly uncultivated towards the west. Continuing on the coast path there is a sense of anticipation as the lighthouse draws ever nearer. Cap Fréhel is spectacular and on its eastern side the path along the cliff-top affords a clear view towards St-Malo, with the occasional ferry catching the sun across the shimmering water. Closer to hand, guillemots weave in and out of the granite stacks of the *fauconière* (falconry). The last section around the bay of Les Sévignés has Fort La Latte as the goal, now sunlit, now in shade with each passing cloud. A visit to the fort is definitely in order when it's open, if not there is still one last spectacle - the finger of Gargantua on the way up to the car-park. (Don't forget the binoculars.)

DIRECTIONS

1. From car-park turn L and go back up road • 200m take first R • Follow through hamlet of La Latte • At cross-roads CA • Pass to R of farm (selling goat's cheese) **• At track TJ turn L • At road go R • At TJ go R • In centre of La Ville Menier bear L and CA on track • 500m, and 50m short of road, turn L on another track • At track TJ bear R • At track joining from left CA • At road CA 250m to main road • Bear L on main road**

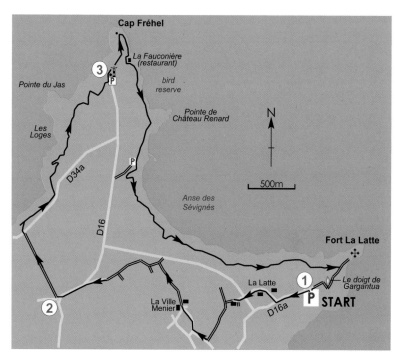

2. At left bend CA into lay-by and turn R onto track (ignore road ahead) • **CA 750m** • **Cross road and CA on path, bearing R to join coast path** • **Follow towards Cap Fréhel** (lighthouse)

The coast path is well marked (red and white) and with the occasional map for orientation. Much of the way, particularly across Cap Fréhel, is bordered by a low wire fence. Please keep to the path and keep dogs under control as this is a natural habitat for wildlife. Apart from the usual gulls, one can expect to see guillemots, razorbills and, with luck, peregrine falcons.

3. From the lighthouse and car-park, CA to the point (little round tower) **and return along other side to restaurant** (La Fauconière) • **CA on coast path all the way to Fort La Latte** • **At access road to fort turn R and follow up to car-park,** passing menhir on right, Gargantua's finger

OTHER WALKS in the area:
Erquy (16kms W) A 9½km circuit of cliffs and coves around the Cap d'Erquy (see Walking Brittany, Walk No.16).

PLACES OF INTEREST nearby:
Fort La Latte (on route) Guided visits - open every day Easter to end of September, mornings and afternoons; rest of year - weekends, public and school holidays, afternoons only.

WALK 36: Evran

Length 15 kms	Time 5 hrs	Level 2

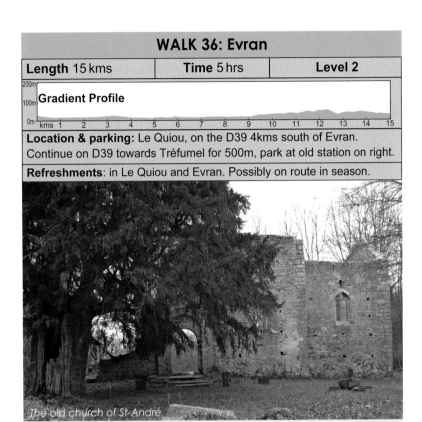

Gradient Profile

Location & parking: Le Quiou, on the D39 4kms south of Evran. Continue on D39 towards Tréfumel for 500m, park at old station on right.

Refreshments: in Le Quiou and Evran. Possibly on route in season.

The old church of St-André

A long walk but with a variety of interest including railways, birds, ruined churches, canals, a Roman road and a villa, old lime-kilns, geology, and a château.

DIRECTIONS

1. **From old station turn R along former railway track-bed** This was the standard gauge line that linked La Brohinière and the Réseau Breton with Dinan, opened in 1896, closed to passengers in 1939 and to freight as late as 1985 • **50m pass site of Gallo-Roman villa on right** • **1150m CA across bridge over river Rance** • **450m CA over track** (near lake on right) • **CA to road** (junction of 3 roads at the old halt of Le Rocher) • **CA on track-bed path** • **400m leave railway, turning R onto rough road and CA** • **300m fork R** • **450m turn L towards church of St-André-des-Eaux** • **Near church, turn sharp R on another track and CA to church** • **CA to road, turn L** • **At main road, cross and CA on path to left of water** • **Follow path near water to ruined church on left** This 11th-15th century ruin used to be the church of St-André-des-Eaux but was so often flooded by the Rance that it was decided in1892 to build a new church on drier land.

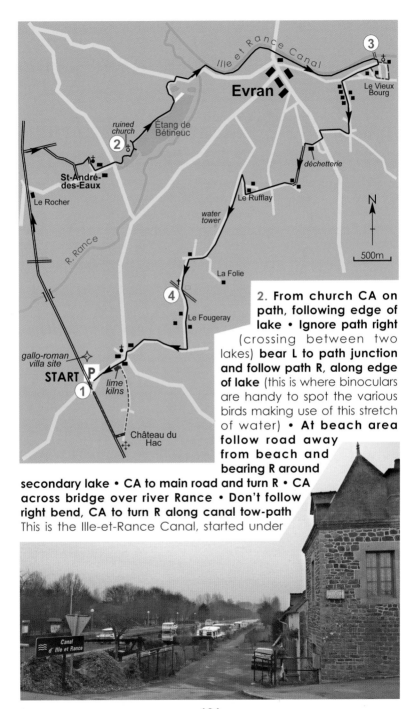

Ille et Rance Canal

Evran

Le Vieux Bourg

ruined church

Étang de Bétineuc

② 2

St-André-des-Eaux

Le Rocher

déchetterie

Le Rufflay

water tower

N

500m

La Folie

④ 4

Le Fougeray

gallo-roman villa site

START P

① 1

lime kilns

Château du Hac

2. From church CA on path, following edge of lake • Ignore path right (crossing between two lakes) **bear L to path junction and follow path R, along edge of lake** (this is where binoculars are handy to spot the various birds making use of this stretch of water) • **At beach area follow road away from beach and bearing R around** secondary lake • **CA to main road and turn R • CA across bridge over river Rance • Don't follow right bend, CA to turn R along canal tow-path** This is the Ille-et-Rance Canal, started under

Canal d' Ille et Rance

Napoleon in 1804 and completed in 1832. It meets the river Vilaine at Rennes, thus linking St-Malo with the Nantes-Brest Canal at Redon, and the Atlantic • **At bridge in Evran, cross road and CA on tow-path as before** A notice on the corner of the building opposite recalls that navigation was interrupted by drought in June 1921 and was not resumed until February 1922

3. At iron footbridge, turn R away from canal 40m to road

Diversion: turn L to ruined church in Le Vieux Bourg and take a circular tour of the old village This was the administrative and religious centre of the *commune* of St-Judoce until the beginning of the 20th century. The disused church dates from the 12th century.

Main route: **turn R and CA 400m to main road • Cross main road and CA down road opposite • CA 700m through houses to cross-roads • Turn R • At main road turn L • Take 1st R** (signed to *la Déchetterie*) • **At *déchetterie* bear R and CA on footpath** (between two wooden posts) • **At road turn L • CA on track • 500m in hamlet follow R to little road and follow that R • At cross-roads CA** (signed Le Rufflay) • **Ignore road right but CA and follow R • At TJ turn L • CA past water tower (good views) • Bear R** (past left turn to La Folie) • **In hamlet ignore right turn • 50m turn L** (signed to Le Fougeray)

Le Rufflay

4. At hill-top - pumping station on left, cross and shrine on right, line of Roman road going across and down right side of pumping station This is the Roman road from Corseul (*Fanum Martis)* to Rennes (*Condate)* • **CA on road 800m to TJ and turn R • CA 850m into Le Quiou • At TJ opposite church turn L and immediately R down D39 to station**

Diversion: take 1st turn L (signed Château du Hac) and CA 950m to château gates. Here turn R down to railway track-bed and follow R, back to station. The Château du Hac was built between 1440 and 1448 by Jean Hingant, a courtier who acquired the *domaine* from Arthur de Richemont (later Duke Arthur III). In 1450, Hingant lost his possessions through being too closely involved in the murder of Gilles de Bretagne and the château passed to the Tournemines (see p.82). The château has been altered little since it was built and is a fine example of 15th century noble architecture. Still privately owned, it is open to visitors in August and September, afternoons only. It contains a collection of period furniture, notably chests, four-poster beds and tapestries.

Main route: **on left after diversion turning is a former lime kiln**, built in 1892 to take advantage of the local geology. Rich deposits, sometimes chalky, sometimes of sedimentary limestone (*pierre de jauge*) are the result of layers of sea shells from the warm, shallow Falun sea that separated western Brittany from the Paris basin in the Tertiary period, 15 million years ago. The kilns were closed down in 1972 and their quarry nearby is now flooded.

Lime kilns at Le Quiou

OTHER WALKS in the area:

Les Champs Géraux (4½ kms N of Evran) Starting from the Salles des Fêtes, a rural circuit of 10-12kms goes to the west and northwest of the *bourg*.

PLACES OF INTEREST nearby:

St-Juvat and **Tréfumel** (2kms W and SW from Le Quiou) Their architectural richness has earned them the title '*communes du patrimoine rural*'.

Index of places

other RED DOG books

Explore Brittany

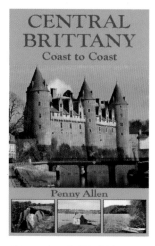

Walking Brittany
by Judy Smith

28 walks covering spectacular coast, hills and forests, varied water courses and traditional countryside. The text includes full directions and provides atmospheric accounts of places of interest on the routes - megalithic monuments, châteaux and sacred structures with their associated legends.

ISBN: 978 0 9536001 4 4

£9.95   15€00

Central Brittany
Coast to Coast
by Penny Allen

The key to a landscape alive with legend and places of historic significance. Covers a north to south section of Brittany from the pink granite coast to the Gulf of Morbihan. Also included is a selection of detailed scenic walks with full directions and points of interest.

ISBN: 978 0 9536001 6 8

£8.99   13€50

www.reddogbooks.com

other RED DOG books

Explore Brittany

Walking the Brittany Coast

Experience Brittany's 1200 kms of spectacular coastline on foot

These volumes present the essence of Brittany's coast - rugged cliffs, sandy beaches, wooded estuaries, exposed headlands, sheltered coves, ports large and small, islands, and the ever present sea

- Full directions for walkers • Places of interest described
- Beautiful colour photographs • Historic, cultural & economic features
- Planning for walking holidays / short breaks
- Accommodation, refreshments, transport
- Suggestions for circular walks

Vol 1: Mont St-Michel to Morlaix	Vol 2: Morlaix to Benodet
by Judy Smith	by Wendy Mewes
ISBN 978 0 9557088 0 0	ISBN 978 0 9557088 1 7
£9.95 15€00	£9.95 15€00

www.reddogbooks.com

other RED DOG books

Discover Brittany

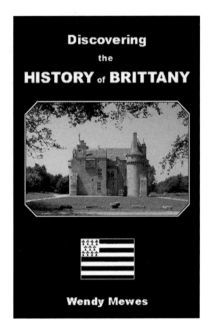

Discovering the History of Brittany

by Wendy Mewes
A concise account of the history of this extraordinary
region. It offers a clear picture of a complex subject
through the presentation of people and places that
have coloured events from pre-historic times to the
present day. Colour photographs and line drawings
illustrate many aspects of Brittany's historical heritage.

ISBN: 978 0 9536001 5 1

£8.99   13€50

www.reddogbooks.com